An Extravagance of
Donkeys

Janet Baker-Carr

iUniverse, Inc.
New York Lincoln Shanghai

An Extravagance of Donkeys

iUniverse books may be ordered through booksellers or by contacting:

iUniverse
2021 Pine Lake Road, Suite 100
Lincoln, NE 68512
www.iuniverse.com
1-800-Authors (1-800-288-4677)

ISBN-13: 978-0-595-38855-4 (pbk)
ISBN-13: 978-0-595-83235-4 (ebk)
ISBN-10: 0-595-38855-8 (pbk)
ISBN-10: 0-595-83235-0 (ebk)

Printed in the United States of America

An Extravagance of
Donkeys

Contents

ACKNOWEDGEMENTS

I am most grateful to the following people who have graciously helped me in the preparation of this book: Fran Chilcote, Ron Chilcote, Ellen Cooper Klyce, Ted Rust and Melissa Stroud. Their help has been in the form of editorial advice, technical assistance and careful proofreading! As much as these skills are truly appreciated, I thank them above all for their enthusiasm for this project.

My gratitude also goes to my friends at Trezevant Manor in Memphis, Tennessee who invited me to read these stories to them not once but twice!

Thank you all!

PREFACE

On December 4, 1984, my husband, Herb Agoos, and I changed our lives in a way we had not anticipated. Highland Farm in East Andover, New Hampshire, had come up for sale during the previous summer. In 1934, Herb's father had bought the farm and used it as a retreat from his demanding business life in Boston. After his death, Herb's sister and her husband bought the farm, and finally it was sold out of the family in the 1960s.

Bringing it back into the family was certainly appealing in a romantic way, but our final decision came when we learned that a developer was interested in building multiple small dwellings on the beautiful hillside pasture behind the house and its noble barn.

Herb was retired and his children were grown, leading their own lives. My daughters were in graduate school and college, and I thought I could find a job nearby. We felt free to move from Cambridge, Massachusetts, where we had been living, and so we did.

When we arrived at Highland Farm on that snowy fourth of December, two things struck us as remarkable. In the empty room above the garage there was a makeshift table on which lay a copy of *The Saturday Evening Post* from the 1940s. The cover proudly announced a Young Ames story written by Walter D. Edmonds. He was my stepfather. And, when we opened the linen closet, there was a towel neatly folded, never used, which bore the monogram of Herb's mother. It must have been sitting there for some forty years. Were these signs of welcome?

Highland Farm's handsome eighteenth century farmhouse stood in sharp contrast to the contemporary house Herb had built just down the hill on Highland Lake in the 1940s. With its dihedral roof and expansive glass exterior, it could not have been more different from the historic farmhouse.

Herb was pleased to be at both houses and, until he was no longer able, took great joy in keeping both looking beautiful. Herb had always loved New Hampshire, and so he was pleased to be there permanently. Initially we thought we would keep a tiny apartment in Cambridge, but we didn't. We were where we wanted to be.

My special delight in being at the farm came from the opportunity to return to rural life. Since I had come to this country in December 1948, I had lived in both Cambridge and New York City. My childhood had been spent surrounded by a variety of animals deep in rural England.

Filling the barn at Highland Farm with donkeys came swiftly. I don't think I realized it at the time, but I wanted to offer a safe haven to donkeys whose families had no use for them any longer. The phrase "donkey's years" is only partially correct. Initially the phrase was "donkey's ears," which are long, but donkeys often do live long lives and children progress to other interests as they grow up, yet the donkey lives on, often feeling lonely and neglected. After the terrible, sad death of our donkey in England, I wanted to be sure that it wouldn't happen again.

Herb liked the idea of animals in the barn and he liked to see the donkeys grazing on the hillside. He was interested in them but not involved in their daily care, preferring just to keep company as we walked in the woods. Though he kept his distance, he took great pleasure in my happiness and enjoyed my delight and love for these appealing animals.

What a surprise it must have been for the unsuspecting motorist coming up the winding road from the village of East Andover to see twelve to fourteen donkeys and a mule grazing peacefully on the hillside. Often, a car would stop and out would come a camera. If I were with the donkeys, there would be the inevitable question, "Why donkeys?"

"I just like them," I'd say. But there was more to it than that. The story of my love for donkeys begins in England.

1

WHY DONKEYS?

Like many families who lived in rural England, we had a donkey. Two donkeys. I don't remember the first. Old Joe came from the top of Box Hill where there was a spectacular view of the Wye Valley, and on weekends families came to picnic and to admire the view. For a penny a child could ride one of several donkeys. Old Joe had been giving rides to children for many years. He'd walk slowly in a large circle while the child either loved it or hated it. It didn't matter which to Old Joe. When he had completed the circle the child would be removed and another put on.

I think my parents took pity on Old Joe and offered him a quiet retirement in our pleasant pasture where he could rest in the shade of the ancient oak trees. Sometimes my sister and brother and their friends had rides. Old Joe never forgot his duty. He'd walk slowly and carefully in a big circle and then stop. The child would have to be replaced by another or get off and be put on again before Old Joe would start once more. We had him for about a year. One night he lay down to sleep and never woke up.

Just when Jenny came I don't know, and I don't know where she came from. She was young and spirited and she was my first memory. I remember that I had on scratchy pink leggings, and I recall being lifted on to her soft furry back and given a ride. I must have been two. For the next few years I think that is how we spent our afternoons. Following a nap and before tea, my older sister, Sally, and I would sit on Jenny as Mummy led her through winding country lanes. My brother, Christopher, rode his bike beside us, complaining no doubt about how slow we were.

Those bucolic meanders came to an abrupt end in 1939 with the beginning of WW II. Then my mother spent many afternoons at the big table in my bedroom with our neighbor, Rachael, sewing the heavy blackout curtains for each window of our respective houses. It was a long and arduous task. Rachael's daughter Sue, who was my best friend, sat under the table with me playing house. Once I heard my mother say, "I wonder what we will use these for when the war is over."

"If we are still alive," said Aunt Rachael."

"Shush," said my mother quickly, "the children will hear." From then on the sewing session conversations took on a happier tone.

The war effort became an appropriate obsession for all of us. Even Jenny was enlisted. My mother heard about a goat farm where Jenny was sent to help hauling bags of feed and plowing fields. But Jenny did not share my mother's view of patriotism. Put in a field with nothing but goats for company, Jenny chased and nipped them. She also refused to be caught. Finally after several months she was sent home.

Donkeys' hooves grow quickly and instead of chipping pieces off like a horse's hoof, they curl up so that the donkey is thrown off balance and walks on the soft tender heel in excruciating pain. Poor Jenny could hardly walk when she came home. The Land Girls at the farm next door put her in a cart pulled by Prince, the large black workhorse, and drove her in style to the blacksmith. It took several months for her hooves to return to their normal shape. But it was more than her hooves that were affected. The entire experience left Jenny angry and vicious. With her head down and her teeth bared, she chased anyone who went into her field. Mummy said "Oh, leave her alone, she'll get over it." But she didn't.

One day I went in her field and was duly chased out. I tried again and once more she chased me. The third time I didn't run. I just stood still. Jenny hurled herself toward me. I can still feel her hot breath on my face as she skidded to a halt inches from me. I must have been six at the time.

From then on we were inseparable. With Sue on her pony, we went for long rides in Deepdene woods at the entrance of which Romany gypsies lived in discarded railway carriages. They looked so strange sitting in the seats peering out the windows as if they were traveling to London. The paths through the woods were complicated and often we were lost. But we never worried. I'd just drop the reins on Jenny's neck and say "Jenny, let's go home." She would lead us out quickly.

My mother was only a little surprised one day when she woke from her nap on the living room couch to find Jenny looking down at her. I had brought her in for tea. It was a short visit. A few days later when Mummy went to town grocery shopping, I brought Jenny in again. This time, with no grownup around, Jenny wandered freely through the living room, dining room, and into the kitchen. There she solemnly ate an apple. Then she went upstairs. We lived in an Elizabethan farmhouse and the staircase was spiral. Jenny went up happily and, always curious, she found her way into the bedrooms and even the bathroom, which didn't interest her. About that time I thought my mother could be coming and that I ought to get Jenny back in her field. At the top of the stairs she stopped dead. I pushed her and she leaned back. I pulled her and she threw up her head in defiance. I tried to bribe her with an apple. No luck. Finally in desperation I got my favorite cardigan, put her ears in the arms and buttoned it up over her face so she could not see. With gentle urging she took the first step and quickly, establishing her own rhythm, she clattered down. Both the cardigan and the donkey were back where they belonged when the car came up the driveway shortly after.

Jenny wasn't always so amenable. Using the wheels of an old pram and a big wooden box, I made a little cart for her to pull. I even put on a dress so we would travel in style. Poised at the side of the road, I urged Jenny forward. She lurched to the left, tipping me and the cart into the ditch. Pulling herself free, she galloped triumphantly back to her field, kicking and bucking.

We lived about twenty-five miles south of London in what is known as the Green Belt. Nothing can be built there or altered. The verdant countryside remains beautiful and unspoiled to this day. In the Blitz and the Battle of Britain, the Luftwaffe flew over on their way to bomb London. Sometimes they dropped their bombs early. Often there were "dog fights" in the sky above us where RAF pilots attacked German planes.

Each night at 7:30, after she had tucked us in bed, my mother went downstairs and played her cello. Softly at first, then increasingly louder, she played music that I was only later in life able to identify by name. Close to eight o'clock she always played the Prelude to Bach's Third Suite for Unaccompanied Cello. It was powerful and full of bite, I knew it was close to eight because it was then that we heard the air raid siren and the menacing, heavy drone of the German planes as they flew over on their way to London. As I lay in bed listening to her play, it was clear to me that my mother was trying to hold off the planes, hoping that tonight her music would change the relentless routine—that her music would keep her family safe.

When the air raid was over and we were back from the shelter and in our beds once more, my mother went downstairs, this time to the piano. She played Schumann and Chopin quietly, gently, and I wondered if she were crying. One night she woke us up again at about three in the morning and took us up to the attic window looking north. There was a huge orange glow in the sky. "That's London burning," she said, "don't ever forget you saw it."

After a night of fierce dogfights, with many planes hit and crashing to the ground, Jenny and I went for a ride in the field below the farm next door. It was a pretty field with a stream quietly running down one side and thick woods where the path ended. As we came close to the woods, Jenny stopped suddenly and threw up her head, and I saw, as she had, a German pilot hiding in the underbrush. Jenny turned sharply and headed back up the path towards home at a brisk canter, much faster than her usual pace.

I had seen the expression on the pilot's face once before when I was smaller. I had been sitting on the swing at the end of the garden when the foxhunt was underway with horses galloping, hunting horn blowing, and hounds in full tongue racing across the field beside me. A slight movement caught my eye in the ditch beside me. It was the fox panting and terrified, wild-eyed pleading for his life. I never told anyone about the German pilot. For a long time I was also frightened that he would climb in my bedroom window and kill me.

Once I entered Jenny into several events at a Pony Club Gymkhana. We didn't win any prizes, and the closest we came to disaster was when Jenny decided to walk under the stomach of the large pony standing next to us in the ring. Jenny fit under but I had to jump off fast. Someone gave me five shillings as a sportsmanship award, and Jenny ate ice cream cones given her by the man in the van who was selling them. "Blimey, a donkey wot eats ice cream. Now I've seen everthin'!"

Anytime Jenny had had enough of being ridden, she headed back to her field and the patch where she liked to roll. First she rolled, and then she lay groaning and breathing hard. Finally she held her breath, always long enough for me to be terrified and scream, "Quick Mummy, Jenny's dead." Invariably my mother would stick her head out an upstairs window, "Jenny, shame on you, get up." And Jenny would jump up looking as close to embarrassed as a donkey can.

It was easy to fall off Jenny, and I often did. She'd suddenly swerve and off I'd go. Or she would go under a low branch and off I'd go again. Twice I broke my arm but that was more a function of poor diet in the war than anything else. What it did mean, however, was that for eight weeks and then ten weeks my arm was in a cast, I wasn't allowed to ride. At those times we were just friends going for walks. I'd brush her or just sit with her in the field while she grazed or slept. She was comfortable to lean against when she lay down to rest. She seemed to welcome my presence.

When the war was over and following my parents' divorce, my mother decided to return to her native America. She brought my sister and me with her. My brother was old enough to choose to stay in England. I was thirteen when we left England, and the memory remains a blur of anger and anguish.

We gave Jenny and my dog Benny to the local vicar's family, whom we knew well. There were six children and they all liked Jenny who had on several occasions spent a week or so in their field when we were away. She knew we would always come back and take her home. At the center of their field stood an oak tree for shade, and it had a swing, a rope for climbing and a tire hanging for the children to play and swing on.

Just a year after we left, a letter came from the vicar saying that when he had gone out to the field that morning to give Jenny some hay, he had found her dead, hanging with her head and neck stuck through a tire. She had pushed her head so far through that she had strangled. Had she been a person her death would have been ruled "an apparent suicide."

I spent my childhood with Jenny. Those memories remain vivid and precious. It must have been that strong bond that made it so natural for me to fill the barn at Highland Farm with those gentle, responsive, and companionable animals.

2

THE BARN AT HIGHLAND FARM

Situated high on a hill and overlooking a lake, the barn is a monument to another time. More than a hundred feet long and standing four stories tall, it is a cathedral, testament to the soaring hopes of the region's earliest settlers.

It was built in 1792 and was the work of many hands and strong backs, as well as teams of patient oxen who pulled huge granite boulders and heavy timbers that are the barn's support structure. The barn is white with dark green trim and has heavy sliding doors that open the north and south ends of the long nave. Floorboards, three deep, are strong enough to carry three pickup trucks end to end and piled high with bales of hay to be thrown to the upper levels and stacked neatly for use during the winter. In the earliest times loose hay was brought by horse drawn wagons and was lifted by great iron claws and a rope-pulley up through the top window and dropped inside.

At the top of the barn is a twelve-foot square cupola with four tall arched windows. Well-worn rungs climb up one side of the nave to reach the cupola where itinerant workers slept during the haying seasons long ago. Outside, on top of the cupola, a handsome bull stood on the weather vane for almost two hundred years as if directing the passage of wind. Two centuries of storms have moved the weather vane's axis so that north points east. The bull is large enough to hold seven crows on his back and one on his head. Still splashed with white, the bull now proudly hangs over the fireplace in the living room, safe from thieves who, using helicopters, steal such priceless objects.

Three sides of the barn rest on huge granite boulders harvested from the surrounding fields. Throughout each floor heavy timbers support the central structure. The lowest floor is used for storing farm equipment and at its northeast end there is an area where animals can come in for shelter. From there a ramp leads up through a door into the main floor where the stalls are and where the animals spend the night in winter.

Not much has changed within the barn over the years. Some heavy guy wires between beams on the second level have been added to insure the barn's integrity, and some poured concrete has shored up one side of the lowest level where supporting boulders had begun to shift.

On the west side of the nave is one long area almost the entire length of the barn and twenty feet wide. That is where the stanchions were that housed a herd of milking cows. Now it is where the donkeys live. On the other side of the nave are seven oversized box stalls where oxen and teams of heavy workhorses used to live. I use the stalls for sheep, nurseries for baby donkeys, a tack room, and for my daughter Harriet's Arabian mare, Phoeba. There is also one stall that is filled with wood shavings that are used for bedding.

The nine-acre pasture around the barn stretches up the hillside to the woods beyond. At one time the field was part of the apple orchard. In 1938 all but three trees were blown down in the hurricane that swept through New England with no warning, washing out roads and devastating the region's crops and trees. Of the three trees that remain, two are behind a pile of rocks and were probably protected by it at the time of the storm. The third must have survived by a fluke. Near the pond it leans to the east, its branches pointing skyward more like a pear tree than an apple. One fall day I counted seventeen bluebirds gathered in its upturned branches. In a single breathtaking, shimmering iridescence they flew up heading due south for winter. Each year the tree bears small inedible, hard apples. But when they ferment and fall off in winter, the donkeys gobble them up, no doubt welcoming their brief buzz of distilled warmth.

The tract of land that originally made up Highland Farm was close to two thousand acres and was shared by two brothers. The older, William Batchelder, took the northern half, for he felt there were not enough rocks in the southern half to build stonewalls around his pastures. The younger brother took the southern half and found stones enough for his walls and an additional supply at the center of the field behind the barn. That pile of granite rock, thirty feet square and three feet high, holds the warmth of the summer sun until late October.

But what of the procession of animals and farmers who have used the barn during its two hundred years? I wonder about them but know little. John Graves moved with his family to the cottage across the road from the farm in 1934 and until the early 1960s farmed the land and used the barn for his cattle and sheep as well as his team of horses. But his main operation became chickens. John had thousands of chickens housed in a tall green barn next to his house. When we first came to the farm, John, who was then in his late eighties, said sadly, "I expect you won't want me to be going in the barn anymore." We reassured him that we expected him to keep his tractors and other equipment under the barn as he always had and to go in whenever he wanted. Early each morning John walked purposefully over to the barn and disappeared inside. I have no idea what he did. Perhaps he just needed to feel the peace of that extraordinary space, to smell the hay and to have his own quiet memories. I think the barn was one of the guy wires of his existence.

When I brought animals to the barn, John would talk to me while I wheeled barrows of manure and swept each morning. First, like many people, he did not understand my affection for the donkeys, but after a while he seemed to understand and took some pleasure in their lives. Perhaps it was that after more than twenty years of being used only for storage, the barn had come back to life with warm animal smells and sounds.

Frail at eight-eight, John died in his ninety-first year. He just faded away, but I feel his presence still.

Nahum and Solomon were the first two donkeys that came to the farm. They had been together for the previous twenty-six years, nearly all of which had been spent at a gentleman farm in eastern New Hampshire. We adopted them from the daughter who needed to sell the property in order to settle her parents' estate.

When Nahum and Solomon first arrived, Harriet exclaimed, "Mom, those aren't donkeys, they're coffee tables." They were heavy! Brian, the vet, agreed but said they seemed healthy for their age, if overweight. He also said that Nahum seemed older, and he was not sure how long he might live. It was Brian's suggestion that I get another donkey so that if Nahum died, Solomon would not be lonely. And that is how my extravagance of donkeys began.

I made some inquiries and heard about two small females for sale in Connecticut. But before I had time to get them, a neighbor told me that an elderly couple he knew needed to find a home for their two donkeys.

As I drove home with them in the horse trailer behind my truck, it occurred to me that Nahum and Solomon had not seen other donkeys for twenty-six years. They stood at the gate and watched as I let down the back of the trailer and led Jenny and Nicholas out. Nahum and Solomon fled to the farthest end of the paddock where they started to bray. It was a loud raucous sound, and they kept it up, sides heaving with exertion and indignation. Completely ignoring the noise, Jenny rolled in the grass and began to graze. Nicholas stood transfixed and shaking. He was breathing hard, and his head was held high. There were cows in the next field. Clearly, he had never seen one before.

The four donkeys spent the remainder of the day getting used to each other. There was plenty of squealing and braying, snorting and trotting about. The next morning they filed out of the barn one behind the other led by Solomon, and they grazed peacefully as if they had been together for years.

Two days later I drove to Connecticut and brought back two small gray donkeys, Molly with a white muzzle and Madeline with a black one. All four donkeys greeted them at the gate with curiosity and interest. All six cantered around the field kicking up their hooves, stopping every once in a while to roll and eat. It went on late into the night—the silent procession of cantering donkeys, moving like ghosts around and around the field.

Brian came to check the four new donkeys, and as he looked at them wandering about, he was startled by the change in Nahum and Solomon, but particularly Nahum. Both donkeys had slimmed down considerably, and they looked alert and vital. Brian was delighted. "I wouldn't have believed such a change could happen so fast. Those two will probably outlive the rest," he said.

Although the hurricane of 1938 roared through New England unannounced and devastating, there was ample warning in 1986 for hurricane Gloria. As she made her way up the mid-Atlantic coast, people of the Northeast had time to prepare. We had just received a delivery of wood shavings that were to serve as bedding for the winter. The delivery was made by a fourteen-wheel dump truck that backed up to the southern entrance to the barn. Lisa, the woman who drove the truck, deposited the load just inside with great precision. When I closed the heavy sliding door, not one wood shaving remained outside. It usually took me two or three days to move the huge pile of shavings into the large stall where they were easily available each day.

On my way to the barn on the morning that Gloria was scheduled to hit New Hampshire, I saw the donkeys huddled under trees at the top of the pasture. They looked miserable. Their heads were down, and their ears hung sideways so the heavy rain couldn't drip inside. They ignored my first call, but by the third they started toward the barn. Slowly at first, then picking up speed, they cantered down the hill. Under the barn they found I had opened the door at the top of the ramp so they came up bedraggled, wet, and not a little surprised at this change in their routine, I closed the door behind them. I had already closed all the other outside doors. The donkeys followed me into the nave of the barn where the huge pile of wood shavings lay, and from there they found they had access to the entire barn. They wandered about enjoying their sudden freedom.

Gloria turned out to be less than a hurricane, but the old barn creaked and sighed with the heavy winds and rain beating against it. It was a comforting isolation. All day and into the evening the donkeys and I listened to the sounds of the storm. As I shoveled shavings from one place to another I mused about other people and other animals before us who had also been grateful for the protection of this great barn.

The donkeys seemed not to notice the storm. They found small caches of ancient hayseed behind old beams. They rolled on the wide floorboards. They groomed each other with their teeth. They slept. They watched me, curious about what I was doing. Nahum, one of the small donkeys, made his way up the pile of shavings and relieved himself. He knew what shavings were for.

High above our heads, Miss Pocket, my daughter Harriet's pitch-black cat, moved silently across the highest beams. Light from the naked bulbs below threw the shadow of a huge wild beast behind her on the wall. My old city cat, Mozart, sat on a high shelf in mesmerized disdain, but poised for flight as he watched the donkeys below.

How quickly the barn had come to life when the animals arrived. When I had walked into the barn for the very first time, I was awed by its size, by its structure and by its serenity. It was a holy place and like a cathedral on a Monday, it cried out for life. The sheep, mules, donkeys, and horses have made it glow the way a beautifully appointed house does. The barn is grateful for the animals and the people who use it.

In our years at the farm there have been births and deaths in it. And then there was Jenny. She must have been close to fifteen years old when she came, but like all the donkeys that came to Highland Farm Jenny took a new lease on life, becoming both playful and affectionate as well as healthier. One day Harriet and I had taken a large brown paper bag out to the field filled with carrots. When the carrots were gone, we watched as Jenny put her head in the bag and then walk around with it over her head. Clearly, she was pleased with herself. We got more bags and soon the entire herd was walking around with bags over their heads. We couldn't imagine what the attraction was, but it was a comical parade.

Willi, a dashing young male donkey, came to stay at the farm so that we might have some baby donkeys. I was sure that Jenny and Annie were too old to give birth but there were three young females who could. After ten months Jenny looked heavier and seemed to move more slowly. Harriet and I were sure that she was in foal. The gestation period for a donkey is thirteen months. Closer to the time, Brian, the vet, gave me some iodine and cotton to cleanse the foal's navel and told me to call him when Jenny went into labor. Amy, our doctor and neighbor made me promise to call her. She said she had never delivered a four-legged creature. And so we waited.

Jenny seemed really quite heavy, her bag for milk swelled. We made a special stall for her at night away from the other donkeys. She lay on the shavings in her private abode like a queen. Finally, Harriet and I decided we should sit outside her stall after dark so we could hear her when she went into labor. We took mugs of tea and sat on the floor outside the stall and whispered to each other choosing names. Would it be gray like Willi or white like Jenny? And how do you help a donkey give birth?

Jenny groaned. She groaned again. Silently Harriet opened the door. By the light of the flashlight we could see Jenny lying on her side breathing hard. Harriet whispered, "Call Brian, I'll stay here." "Congratulations!" said Brian. "I'll be over first thing in the morning to give it a look over and a tetanus shot." Once again he gave me clear instructions about iodine and the navel, and keeping the afterbirth for him to see, "But call again if you need help," he finished.

Forgetting to call Amy, I ran back to the barn. The lights were on and Harriet, hearing footsteps, came out to meet me. "Come and see," Harriet said with an odd grin. Jenny was standing up and eating hay. I looked for the foal. There wasn't one.

"What happened?" I asked.

"Well," said Harriet, "she groaned a couple more times, then as if she had woken from a nightmare, she scrambled to her feet. Now she is eating hay."

We were both stunned. It was hard to accept what had not happened. Harriet said quietly, "Mom, I don't think Jenny was ever pregnant."

Brian confirmed it the next morning. He checked her over carefully. "We don't really know why a false pregnancy occurs, but they do, don't they Jenny." He patted her kindly.

Later that year Harriet got married and went to live in Mississippi. She took Miss Pocket with her and Phoeba, the beautiful Arabian mare she had trained herself. If Miss Pocket missed prowling the highest beams in the barn, she never showed it. She settled in to her new home quickly, glad to be with Harriet and Stephen. Phoeba had a more difficult time. Being an Arab she was able to tolerate the intense heat with little effect but the fierce thunderstorms that are so prevalent in the Deep South threw Phoeba into a panic, and she developed colic each time. Not only were the storms becoming increasingly dangerous to her health, but also they were affecting her easy-going nature.

I received a frantic call from Harriet one night asking me to look after Phoeba at the farm until she found a good home for her.

On the evening Phoeba was scheduled to arrive, I stayed in the barn with all the lights on so the truck driver would know where to come. The donkeys sensed the excitement I felt, and they waited, their heads over the partition of their long stall, their eager eyes looking out into the night. Phoeba arrived at one o'clock in the morning in mid January, and it was the coldest night of the winter so far. She had been on the road for three days in a large horse transport van. The driver stayed for a while to make sure she was all right, and then left to deliver the other horses to Vermont. Phoeba had no reason to grow a heavy coat for winter so she was wearing a blanket. Even with it she started to shiver. It was cold, about fifteen degrees in the barn. Quickly I gave her some grain for instant warmth and then kept her walking to stimulate her circulation. Up and down the center of the barn we went. On the other side of the long partition the donkeys heehawed and kept pace with us. They recognized Phoeba and welcomed her back.

The next morning was cold but sunny. I put Phoeba with the donkeys in the big pasture. As soon as I took off her halter, her nostrils flared and her tail went straight up, being the pure bred she is, she galloped off with that extraordinary gait that Arabian horses have. They seem to levitate as they move hardly grazing the surface of the ground with their hooves. With their heads held high, their manes and tails stream out behind adding to the illusion of weightlessness. Doing their best to keep up with her, the donkeys' short legs moved fast and their hooves pounded the ground beneath them. No two members of the equine family could have looked more different.

Whether it was because her system remembered the climate of the north or just because she was comfortable to be away from the violent storms of the south, I don't know, but Phoeba grew a winter coat almost over night. Finally the cold and snow of winter gave way to spring, and in April with the frost out of the earth, the donkeys lay on the ground once more. I went out to join them as they basked in the first really warm sun of the season. I sat on the ground leaning against old Annie, who always liked company. Phoeba lay in front of me. With a contented sigh, she rolled on her side. Her belly was immense. I found it hard to believe her regular feeding had made her that large.

Later on the phone, I asked Harriet if Phoeba could be in foal. "No," she replied. "She was bred last June but the test was negative and with all the colic and the long trip north, she couldn't be."

"OK," I said, "but I remember feeling the way she looks, slow to get up and slow to go down. We will see."

But Phoeba was not slow in the field. She would suddenly gallop off, her head and tail held high, as she fairly flew around. The blacksmith came to trim all the hooves for spring and I asked Emile what he thought. "Could be," he said. "First time mares are hard to tell. Watch her. She will tell you when it is time." I hoped so. Brian came to give spring shots and said the same thing. He went over the iodine and cotton routine again and told me how important it was for him to see the sack the foal was born in to make sure it had all been expelled. If any of it were to remain in the mare, it could cause her great harm. I listened carefully.

Each day I spent extra time with Phoeba before leading her out in the morning and after she came in from the field at night. She and I had always enjoyed a fine rapport, but I wanted her to feel so safe with me that she would trust me to help her or her foal when it came. I talked to her constantly as time and again I ran my hands over her body, over her belly, up over her hindquarters and down her legs. Sweet Phoeba, she seemed to glow like any mother close to term. Often I sat on the floor in her stall and just kept her company. I had heard of mares that acted strangely after giving birth, some even rejected their foals completely. I wanted to be sure I could handle Phoeba if she needed it.

Early in the morning of May ninth I went into the barn to feed the animals. Usually the donkeys stomp around making sounds of entreaty in anticipation of food, and Phoeba would whinny her welcome. That morning there was not a sound. The donkeys stood silent and solemn. I had seen them like that only once before when one of the sheep had died during the night in a stall across from them. I knew what had happened from the donkeys' faces even before I saw the small, stiff body.

Phoeba was standing on the far side of her stall leaning against the wall. She was drenched in sweat. Speaking to her, I crossed the nave and peered over the partition into her stall. There, in the center, lay a small dark brown body. Its back was toward me. It did not move. Still speaking quietly to Phoeba, I opened the door and on hands and knees moved carefully to where the foal lay. Phoeba looked disoriented and paid no attention to me, but I watched her out of the corner of my eye. My mind raced. How terrible to have to tell Harriet that Phoeba's foal had been born dead. I reached out and put my hand on its back. It was warm. As my hand rested on the soft wet fur, the foal lifted and turned its head so that I found myself looking into its eyes, not two inches from my own. They were deep blue; eyes that held all the innocence that ever was. Involuntary tears ran down my cheeks. Of course, I thought, people greet birth and death in the same way, with tears. Now I know that donkeys greet them both in solemn silence.

Phoeba came over to her foal. She sniffed it curiously. Quickly she and I went about our duties as if we had performed them many times before. She nudged the foal to make it stand and guided it to where the warm milk waited. I swabbed iodine on the navel. Yes, she was a filly. A quick check of both mother and daughter encouraged me to believe all was well. I put the afterbirth in a bucket for Brian.

I marveled at how quickly nature takes care of her own. The lifeless, small brown bundle that I had seen just a few minutes ago was now standing on her tall, thin legs, still unsteady but insisting on her own survival. She suckled her mother's milk noisily. When she stopped, she came over to see what I could offer her. She lifted her face to mine and tried to suck my nose and then my chin. Our eyes met for the second time. This look was different: eager, questioning.

In a mood of jubilation, celebrating the first birth at the farm in my tenure of it, I rolled back the huge door on the south end to let in the sun's light and warmth. My body froze, not twenty feet from the barn was a coyote, the first I had seen. What pungent odor of defenseless vulnerability had this bold predator smelled that encouraged him to sit so smugly, waiting?

"Get away," I yelled, and pulled the heavy door shut. In the safety of the barn, Phoeba and her foal recovered quickly from the trauma of birth. By the third day, they were ready to go outdoors. I put them in the small pasture next to the house. Exhilarated by the warm sun and by being outside again, Phoeba broke into a canter and moved gracefully down the length of the field. The long-legged filly kept pace with her. Around and around the field they went, the epitome of spring. Lined up along the fence that separated the small pasture from the large one, were the donkeys, aunts and uncles all. It was their first full view of the filly, and they trotted back and forth along the fence, braying and snorting their welcome to her. Phoeba lay down and rolled, grunting with pleasure. The small filly snorted, jumping and twisting her body as she experimented with new ways to move. Later in the afternoon, I took them back to their stall for the night into the safekeeping of the barn.

From any view, the barn is imposing in its magnitude. It is a sanctuary for its inhabitants. The farmers who lived in this house previously must have rested peacefully at night as we do, knowing their precious livestock was safe from storms and predators. On cold winter nights when the ground is covered with snow and the moon is bright, I look out of our bedroom window and marvel at the silhouette of the great barn with its deep tranquil shadows, and I am awed once more by the ambition and industry of those early settlers who built it.

3

MAGGIE, FRED AND MUPO THE MULES

The woods that bound the farm's northern property line stretch northwest for countless acres. Through them wind narrow footpaths, bridle trails and old rutted logging roads that lead over steep terrain to small villages, some as far as several miles away. One of my favorite paths follows a small tributary of Mountain Brook, which flows through a steep and densely wooded area for close to a mile. After clambering up an unforgiving headwall of granite you come to Huntoon Pond. This remote, lovely pond that seems to grace the top of the world was probably made by beavers hundreds of years ago. Now it is the nesting and feeding place for myriad birds that are not disturbed by a solitary visitor.

Huntoon Pond has an aura of mystery about it. Some people doubt that it really exists because it is so easy to get lost while trying to find it. In times past it may not have seemed so remote because near the summit rests an ancient steam engine that might have been used in a logging harvest. Listing to one side and a little forlorn, it sits in the tall grass like a forgotten toy waiting to be picked up and taken home.

It takes many hours to hike to Huntoon Pond and back to the farm. After my first time I looked at the geodesic survey map of the area and saw all the trails and old logging roads I wanted to explore, and I knew that I could not accomplish all I wanted to on my own two feet. I decided that what I needed was a sure-footed, good-natured mule.

In a local paper I found a brief advertisement that read "Clever Mule, $400." I called the number and made arrangements to go the next day to a neighboring village to see her. As we walked to the small barn, her present owner, Hal, told me she had belonged to his recently deceased brother, Art. Hal told me the story of Art's gray donkey, which had been his constant companion for many years and who was quite a character as well as being a local celebrity.

It seems the little gray donkey wandered about as he wished. Each day at four o'clock he trotted down to the local saloon where Art stopped for a beer after work. The little donkey just pushed open the swing door, walked in greeting the other regulars and stood beside Art until it was time to go home. When it came time to leave, the old man and his friend walked home together. Art lived by himself, and the two had followed their daily ritual without variation for many years.

One morning old Art did not wake up. He just died in his sleep. At four o'clock the little donkey trotted down to the saloon as usual. When he did not find his master sitting in his usual place, he became distraught and moved about knocking chairs and pushing tables. The owner called Hal and told him to come and get the donkey and put him in the barn. Hal did, but he said the donkey set up such a bellowing and kicking and banging that Hal did not dare go near him.

Old Art knew his gray friend would not survive well alone. In his will he left $20 to put the little fellow out of his misery. His will also instructed that he and the donkey be buried side by side. So in kindness to one and out of respect to the other, the old friends were laid down together to rest in peace. Hal finished his story, and we walked on in silence. I asked about the mule.

"Maggie." he said with emphasis, "she's clever," and opened the door. The barn was dark inside, and it took a moment for my eyes to adapt. At first I thought I was looking at a moose. Maggie the mule was huge. I had no idea a mule could be that tall.

A mule is a cross between a horse and a donkey. The donkey, a small animal is the father and the horse who is larger is the mother. The physics of Maggie's conception seemed impossible, but in the back of my mind I remembered reading that a donkey uses a winning combination of patience and tenacity. He waits until a large mare lies down to rest or to roll before he makes his purpose clear. Surprise, I thought must play an important part. I would have loved to see the gleam in that small donkey's eye as he surveyed the mare that bore this mule. She must have been the size of a Clydesdale.

"Maggie's clever," Hal said again while he attached a rope to her halter to lead her out. Indeed she was. She put her head down and seemed to buckle at the knees in order to get through the low doorway. Standing outside, I could see she was a beautiful animal. Like most mules she was a rich, dark brown with a black mane and tail. Strong and healthy, she carried herself with pride and she had kind eyes. I ran my hands over her.

"She's gentle, never hurt nothing," Hal said. "Good in the woods too, Just take her up to where the trees are being cut, hook her up to one of them and she'll bring it down to the staging area all by herself. When they unhook her and slap her rump, up she'll go for the next one. Never gets tired. Seems to like the work. Best skidder I ever worked with." He finished.

I'm tall for a woman, close to five-nine, but even so I knew I would have a hard time reaching to the top of her back with a brush. I like to ride bareback. Mules and donkeys have narrow shoulders that make it next to impossible to stay on going down hill. You just slide forward and down the neck. At the top of the hill I usually dismount and walk, remounting at the bottom. Among the hills of New Hampshire there is always a pleasant combination of walking and riding. Sliding off Maggie would not be hard, but how in the woods could I get back up? I also wondered how I would get her the twelve miles home. No one I knew had a trailer that would hold her. In the pasture Maggie would look like the Trojan horse with eight small donkeys around and under her like so many trinkets!

I really liked Maggie. She was a handsome and proud animal. But as I told Hal, she was a little bigger than I had in mind. He seemed relieved and said that he had decided that if I didn't take her, he was going to keep her for himself. "She's a clever one," he said. And I watched her lower her head and buckle her knees as she went through the door back into the small barn.

Fred was a black mule the size of a small horse. He was good-natured and an eager companion in the woods, but he stayed on the farm for two nights and three days. On his arrival, the five female donkeys accepted him almost to the point of ignoring him. However Nahum, Solomon and Nicholas, the three males, refused to leave him alone. First, they tried to drive him off by making rushes at him, heads down, ears flat back and all three attacking at once. Fred just moved off and continued to graze. Then one by one they dive-bombed him, cantering up and trying to bite his legs before they swerved off. For the most part Fred ignored them. He seemed to relish the freedom of the large field and good grazing.

It had not occurred to me that the three male donkeys, all gelded early in their lives, would be so hostile to the gelded mule that clearly had no interest in fighting. The donkeys' aggression was not carried out in silence. Nahum snorted and made a cough-like threat. Solomon, the donkey with the most mellifluous heehaw, brayed his threats and his anger in a sound that ricocheted through the hills and was heard miles away. And he kept it up day and night. I was afraid that Fred's patience would finally run out and that he would turn on the three aggressors. It would have been easy for him to inflict serious injury. So good-natured Fred went back, and Highland Farm returned to its peaceful life.

I bought Mupo sight unseen. She arrived in the back of a pickup truck that had it sides and back made taller with sheets of plywood. She had ridden the one hundred miles north from Boston protected from the wind and from the sight of swiftly moving vehicles going in either direction on Interstate 93. But she had started her trip on Martha's Vineyard, and she must have been startled by the whistles and foghorns and the motion of the ferry and later by the strange odors in the air as she passed through Boston on that steamy hot day in August.

Val, the taller and stronger of the two women who had brought Mupo, removed the truck's back panel. Mupo needed no urging. She jumped down making the whickering sound I was to know so well. She pranced around as if she were testing the ground beneath her. Mupo was beautiful. Smaller than Fred, she looked more like a pony than a mule. She was a pale dappled chestnut with a golden mane and tail. Finely boned yet sturdy, Mupo danced gracefully around me as I led her to the gate where all the donkeys stood waiting. They scattered, snorting as she came into the field. Paying no attention to them, Mupo trotted off a few paces, lay down, and rolled back and forth grunting with pleasure. She got up, shook herself vigorously and then galloped to the back of the pasture. With her long golden tail flowing behind, she fairly floated up the steep hill. The donkeys watched.

While we ate sandwiches on the porch, Val and her friend told us what they knew of Mupo. She was about nine years old and had come from Vermont. It seemed that her original owner was a man who weighed more than two hundred pounds, and he rode her perched on a heavy western saddle. Since she was small and finely boned, the total weight must have strained her brutally. It was said that when he took her coon hunting, he hit her head with a stick in some perverse form of exhilaration. Fortunately, a woman who raised donkeys bought her, and she taught Mupo, or Honey as she was called then, to drive. Mupo proved more than willing. She quickly learned the commands "Gee" and "Haw" for left and right.

Tossing her head in pleasure, she pulled the small sulky proudly through the hilly countryside of Vergennes, Vermont.

Val saw her one day at a donkey and mule club meet, bought her on the spot and took her to Martha's Vineyard. There her name became Mupo, which is short for Mule Pony, the technical name for a small mule. Mupo was the companion of a large donkey, and together they roamed free on the small grass airstrip at Katamah. Now, a year later, Val and her friend were heading west for an extended adventure and were pleased that Mupo would live with the donkeys at Highland Farm. Their own donkey had found a home on the Vineyard.

As they left, Val's friend told us that Mupo was mute. The only sound she ever made was the soft whickering that she had made as she jumped down from the truck. No one had ever heard her bray.

I went out to the field to see the new addition to the herd. Mupo stood up to her knees in mud and water at the edge of the pond, methodically eating the tall green reeds. She seemed oblivious of the semicircle of donkeys that watched. There were eight in all, two black, one white and the rest gray. They knew she was different from them. Being desert animals, no donkey would choose to stand in water. They could see as she flicked flies off her belly with her golden tail that it was a horse's tail, yet she had the dorsal stripe down her back and over her shoulders like a donkey. Her ears were neither horse nor donkey ears, but somewhere between. It was, I suspect, her smell, which told the donkeys what they needed to know. They stood as if transfixed, watching her every move. Every once in a while Solomon, the leader of the herd, lifted his head sideways and brayed. It was not the angry threat he had hurled at Fred, but more chagrin tempered by a query.

Early next morning, I saw all nine animals dozing at the top of the eastern corner of the pasture enjoying the warmth of the early morning sun. Suddenly, without warning or sound, Mupo rounded up the startled donkeys and drove them down the steep hill past the barn, on past the pond, up the rise, and into the upper orchard where they stopped. Mupo put her head down and began to eat the rich thick grass beneath the apple trees while the rest of the herd trotted in circles looking startled.

The run across the pasture was Mupo's expression of dominance. After that she was their leader and they followed her in single file from one part of the field to another and into the barn at night. Solomon was her devoted shadow.

Mupo exceeded all my expectations. Day after day we explored miles of trails that wound through the woods. She seemed as eager for adventure as I was, and no hill or rough terrain dulled her enthusiasm or slowed her pace. Quickly I learned to trust her instincts. She knew when a wet patch was too deep or too boggy to be safe or if a small bridge would or would not hold our weight. She wore a simple bridle with a light bit, and I rode bareback. Our usual pace was a brisk walk, although she liked to trot up hills. Her canter, like all donkeys and I suspect most mules, was hard to sit. Unlike the long graceful motion of a horse, her stride, because of her shorter legs and longer back, was jerky. For the same reason, her trot was different from the bouncy movement of a horse. Mupo's trot was an even running gait, which she could keep up for long stretches and was comfortable to sit riding bareback.

When we left on our expeditions heading down the hill to the old logging road and into the woods, the donkeys walked with us as far as they could on the other side of the fence. When they could go no further at the west corner of the field, we would hear a brief mournful bray of dejection from Solomon. As if by pre-arrangement or intuition, the donkeys were always at the eastern corner of the field on our return many hours later. Amid snorts and their unique gasping sound of pleasure, they walked along the fence beside us up the hill and they fairly danced at the gate to welcome Mupo back.

Mupo would have been a good mother, but mules almost never produce offspring. In the past fifty years, it is said, only two mules had given birth in this country and one in China. It is not that a mule has no estrus cycle; she does and she can conceive. It is the extra chromosome, belonging to neither horse nor donkey, that signals the body to abort an abnormality. There was a moment when I hoped Mupo might deliver a foal. Willi, the jack who came to spend some time at the farm, and Mupo had an exuberant affair, but the months went by and clearly it was not to be.

In another way Mupo may have been just as rare as if she had delivered a foal, for far from being mute, Mupo was bilingual.

Herb and I were in the pasture one morning checking the fence by the road when a horse and rider came up the hill. We had heard that a couple had recently moved into the village and that they had a valuable horse that the young woman rode in cross-country events. It was rare to see a horse and rider go by and certainly a pair so beautiful. The mare's hooves seemed hardly to touch the ground, and she held her head high in eager anticipation of the new surroundings. They halted, and Sue introduced herself and asked about the donkeys that were standing curious and friendly by the fence. The mare bounced sideways and snorted. She was startled to see these small, unfamiliar animals. I looked for Mupo. She was zigzagging down the field at full gallop, her tail streaming out behind her. At the fence she bounced to a stop, turned to face us, and neighed. It was a ragged sound, but it was an unmistakable neigh. The mare lifted her head and neighed in answer. Mupo neighed again, this time more clearly. The mare answered, as Mupo raced across the field, bucking and twisting as if something elemental had been set free.

We never heard her neigh again, but I did hear her bray just once. She and the donkeys were in the barn to have their hooves trimmed by Emile, the blacksmith. It was the first time he had worked on hers so we decided to do her first. She stood perfectly still while Emile cut and rasped each hoof. I gave her a carrot for good behavior and let her out into the field.

The donkeys hate having their hooves trimmed. They don't like being cross-tied, and that makes it worse. Emile worked on the first reluctant donkey while the other seven stood pressed into a corner of the barn trying to hide. A rough raucous heehaw just outside broke the silence. I opened the door, and Mupo burst in and rushed over to stand with her herd.

In the wild, donkeys are prey to large canines and large felines. Attack from a wildcat comes from above. A bobcat or lynx will drop from a tree onto a donkey's back and bite into the large veins in the neck. Attacked in such a way, the donkey pivots a complete circle on its rear hooves and then pulls back. Dazed, the large cat drops to the ground in front of the donkey's head, vulnerable to lethal attack. I have watched a donkey attack a teasing dog. It is quick and final. The donkey grabs the dog's neck in his teeth and breaks its back with sharp powerful front hooves. This instinct even in domesticated donkeys is one reason why they are used with a herd of sheep to protect them from marauding coyotes.

We could never have dogs visit the farm. The donkeys would bray and become aggressive in trying to get at them. But Mupo never seemed disturbed by the presence of a dog. She even continued to graze when five of the gray donkeys herded a fox out of the pasture. In a semicircle around him, they silently drove him up to the top of the field where for a moment he sat on the high stonewall as if to save face. Solomon lunged forward and like fluid the fox drained off the other side and disappeared into the woods.

Late one summer day, I saw a bobcat at the top of the pasture close to where the fox had been. At first I thought he was a large rock that had been displaced somehow from the wall. Then he pounced on his prey, leaving no doubt about his identity. I had never seen one before, and his preoccupation with the rodent gave me time to observe him through binoculars. He was a handsome, healthy bobcat with slightly tufted ears, elegant striping on his face, and a black tip to his stubby tail. Finally, he crouched to eat his kill. I hoped he would stay to wash or even curl up in the sun and sleep. But no, with a graceful leap over the wall he was gone. Mupo and the donkeys were grazing down by the barn and were unaware of the bobcat's visit.

Several days later as I was getting ready for bed, the silence of night was shattered by a terrible scream. The sound was one of alarm and terror, and I knew Mupo had made it. Herb was away at the time. I went downstairs, took the flashlight, and ran into the field. It was a clear, bright night with the moon close to being full, which made it easy to see the silhouettes of the animals. Their heads were high in alert, and they were clearly agitated as they moved nervously, silently through the orchard. Mupo trotted between them. Her neck was arched in tension as she pranced about.

My first thought as I ran out had been an attack by the bobcat. Had he dropped on Mupo from one of the apple trees? I shone the light on Mupo. She was drenched in sweat, but I could not see deep scratches or cuts on her back. The donkeys came toward me, and I spoke to them trying to reassure all of us. Perhaps it had been a bear that had startled Mupo. I hadn't seen any recently but knew they were in the woods.

Mupo stopped in front of me. Her eyes were wild. Instinctively I reached out to calm her. For a fleeting moment she let me touch her, and I felt her whole body quivering. She swerved and raced off snorting. I had hoped she would let me lead her by her forelock into the safety of the barn, but she was too upset. The donkeys clustered around me. If I could get them to follow me, surely Mupo would follow them. Old Annie was next to me. Annie, the vet had said, was closer to forty than she was to anything else. I put my hand under her chin and pulled. She seemed to understand. After a moment's hesitation, she moved forward and, with methodical steps and her chin resting in my hand, we walked toward the barn, followed by the donkeys. Out of the corner of my eye I could see Mupo canter off and then come back to the periphery of the group, canter off and come back. It was an urgent small procession with its nervous outrider. When we reached the barn, I opened the door, and the donkeys pushed their way in. Watching from the door, I waited for Mupo. I could see her eyes flashing in the light from the barn. She circled closer. Finally she came in and I pulled the heavy door shut.

I am frequently amazed by how swiftly and completely donkeys adjust from one situation to the next. As soon as we were away from perceived danger, the donkeys behaved as if I had invited them in for a midnight feast. Smiling at their ebullient demands, I sprinkled a handful of cracked corn on the floor that they ate grain by grain as fast as they could find them.

At first, Mupo, still agitated, paced the barn, and then no longer able to resist the grain on the floor, joined the donkeys. She let me touch her, and she stood still while I brushed her down. All the animals were eating hay contentedly when I finally turned off the barn lights and returned to the house.

The next morning I walked through the orchard looking for any telltale sign of bear or bobcat. I found none. If Mupo had looked up and seen a bear or a bobcat crouched in one of the apple trees, I think she would have made the sound I heard.

Sometimes when I sweep the barn or watch the animals in the pasture, I wonder about Fred and Maggie. I hope Fred is with a family who appreciates his willingness and good nature. And I imagine that Maggie continues to work in Hal's lumber operation and still ducks her head and buckles her knees as she goes in and out of her small barn.

4

BIRDS, BATS AND A BULL

One of my first childhood memories of growing up in England is of our nanny, Mattilda, who had a special love of birds. Mattilda was from Italy, and she was young and cheerful. Every morning before breakfast I watched her go out into the garden and sing softly, calling the birds. One by one they came to her outstretched arms, robins and finches that had always lived in the hedgerows of the garden. Mattilda talked to the birds in Italian, I suppose. There would be four or five on each arm and always one or two on her shoulders, cocking their heads, listening, and chirping.

Some months later World War II broke out, and gentle Mattilda was ordered to leave England, labeled an enemy alien. I remember how she came downstairs with her suitcase packed and her eyes filled with tears.

I did not think about birds much again until I came to Highland Farm some forty-five years later. We passed papers in early December and drove skidding up the steep hill during a snowfall. Soon after the New Year, Herb went to visit his oldest daughter in Australia. In the weeks that followed while Herb was away, I learned the real meaning of "the dead of winter." It was a cold, snowy month with relentless winds from the northwest that blew snow and frigid air continuously. At night the wind shrieked through the space between the house and garage and more than once ripped a shutter off the house.

Sometimes during the day the wind dropped, and snow fell silently, steadily as if to close the earth forever. At those times, even though it was the middle of the day, I would fall into a deep and peaceful sleep. When I ventured out into the large empty barn, the cold was brutal, and the barn had that special dankness that comes from being empty of animals for close to thirty years. There was no sign of life anywhere. It truly was the dead of winter, and I longed to fill the barn with the warmth, sound, and smells of friendly animals.

The first break in the weather came the second week in January and with it the first signs of wild life. Early one morning seven small birds with dark gray backs and white bellies pecked through the cracks in the ice on the driveway trying to glean whatever nourishment they could. I went to the feed store, and bought feeders, a variety of seed, some wire, and hooks. The young man at the counter told me that I could not expect any birds to come this time of year, since I had not begun to feed them in early fall.

Nevertheless, I strung the wire between two young maples outside the porch where I could see them from the kitchen and the bedroom upstairs. Then I filled and hung the feeders. For good measure I sprinkled some seed on the snow-covered ground. At dusk I gave up hope that any birds would come. No doubt the young man had been right.

I opened my eyes the next morning at first light of day not sure what had awoken me. It was the sound of birds. In one of the maples, I counted fourteen evening grosbeaks, noisily scrutinizing the feeders. Within the hour they had emptied them all.

From then on there has been a constant flow of birds to the feeders every day each season. Over time an amazing variety has visited the farm. As the years go by I know which birds will come and when, but none is so precise as the bluebird. The first one arrived on March 26th, a flash of brilliant blue as it flew by me out to the field. I put up a house for it in the pasture where we could see it easily. That summer four baby bluebirds hatched and learned to fly. After the first frost, all six flew south, so we took down the house, cleaned it, and stored it for winter. I put it back up at the beginning of the following March. On March 26th two bluebirds lit on the garage roof, then flew right to their house. That summer there were two babies. The following March, Herb and I were away for a few days at the end of the month, and I forgot to put up the house before we went away. My daughter, Kate, and I were busy talking as we did the dishes after supper. A flash of blue caught my eye as I looked up from the sink. Two bluebirds were perched in the dogwood right outside the window.

"Kate," I said, "Is it the 26th already?"
"Yes, I think it is, why?" she asked.
With flashlight and screwdriver, we put up their little house right then. It has never been late since.

For three summers in a row a great blue heron came to the pond just after three o'clock each day. It landed with great precision and stealthily disappeared amongst the tall reeds at the edge. It stayed for several hours catching small fish and frogs, then took off always in the same flight pattern up over the orchard and off to heaven knows where.

In amongst the iridescent radiance of indigo buntings and goldfinches are siskins, bland and squabbling. In the field, following the donkeys are cowbirds, sedate with their brown heads and shining black bodies. Annie, the oldest of the donkeys, does not mind when one perches on her back as if to hasten the next fall of droppings to be scoured for grain.

As autumn approaches and the air turns cold, the pond becomes a way station for all manner of duck and mergansers as they make their way south. Some stay only a few hours, others remain for many days flaunting their beauteous heads as they feast upon frogs.

Seemingly out of nowhere two turkey vultures appeared one Sunday morning, sitting in the fence near the house. They were close enough that I quickly brought in the two kittens that were playing just outside the door. With their small, naked heads and their menacing stance these huge birds look prehistoric. When they flew off several minutes later, they had to labor hard, in spite of their six-foot wingspan, to gain enough height to clear the trees at the top of the pasture. I have not seen them again.

Starlings nest in one of the ancient maples that grow next to the house. One day I watched in helpless horror as a red squirrel circled the base of the tree. Then with sharp furtive movements he darted up it to return immediately with a fledgling in his mouth. He tore into the flesh of that baby bird's belly devouring it in bloody mouthfuls amid screeches from above. When he finally darted off, all that was left were two little up-turned legs and feet. Higher up that same tree where the starlings nest are two tall dead branches. Almost every morning we hear two pileated wood-peckers banging away at those branches hunting insects. Spectacular black, crow-sized birds with white stripes and flaming red crests, I find them as exciting to see each day as if it were the first sighting.

A loud thump on a window in the porch one morning led me to a little nuthatch that had flown into the window pane and had dropped to the ground below. I picked it up carefully fearing its neck was broken. It was not, and its heart was beating. Sitting on the porch steps, I held it in the palm of my hand to keep it warm. Gently, I stroked its back and spoke to it softly. After a while, the eye, I could see, flickered then blinked slowly. Finally it stayed open, but the little bird still lay motionless in my hand. Then in a moment or so it stood up and stepped onto my index finger, its small feet and claws wrapped around it with a surprisingly strong grip. Whether it stayed for half an hour or three minutes, I have no idea. Time stopped while the nuthatch chose to perch on my finger. I walked over to the tree, thinking it might feel more comfortable in its own surroundings. It stayed, hugging my finger. I walked to the barn, back to the house, and then out to the field talking all the time to the small bird perched on my finger. Then with no warning it let go and flew off.

I suppose I see that bird every day visiting the feeder. I don't know which one it is. But once it gave me the joy of knowing, just for a moment, what Mattilda's daily pleasure must have been.

◆   ◆   ◆

In the middle of one night, I awoke knowing that a bat was swooping around the bedroom. Herb was still away in Australia, or I think he would have caught it. To make matters worse, my cat Mozart, who sleeps at the foot of the bed, was leaping and twirling, trying to catch it. I rolled onto the floor and crouching, opened the door, planning to escape. Instead the bat flew over my head and into the main part of the house with Mozart in close pursuit. I slammed the door shut, jumped back in bed and for the rest of the night sat bolt upright with a sheet tight around my head, watching the windows in case any more should find their way in.

There was no sign of the bat when I went downstairs in the morning, and Mozart was asleep on the couch. When Bill Keyser, our good neighbor from down the hill, came to scrape the barn in preparation for painting, I told him of the bat's visit. To my surprise Bill did not laugh at my fright.

"Bill," I said, "I can't stay in the house tonight with that bat still in there, how can I get it out?" I did not really expect him to have a solution, but he did; one that had worked for him and his wife. Standing high on the ladder, rhythmically scraping off the old paint, he told me not to turn on any lights in the house at dusk and to stay out of the house until after dark. At that point I should park my truck facing the porch door that leads into the kitchen, then open the porch door, turn on the truck's headlights, and wait.

"With any luck, Janet, you'll see that bat float right out the door, drawn by the light," he finished.

After I fed and watered the donkeys that evening, I drove down to Franklin and had dinner at Neil's Restaurant. I ordered a large piece of beef and a beer for good measure.

"Must be a special occasion," said the waitress who I usually asked to bring me much lighter fare.

"Yes, I guess it is," I said smiling ruefully.

Later when I drove up the hill to the farm, the house was pitch dark. I backed the truck under the bird feeders so that it faced the porch door squarely. I opened the porch door so the light would shine right into the kitchen. Then I ran back to the truck and turned the lights on high beam.

Nothing happened. Well, I thought, the bat was probably upstairs and will come down in a minute.

Still nothing.

"Oh, Bill" I said out loud, "it was such a good plan, why isn't it working?"

Still no sign of the bat, and I had visions of sleeping in the truck. Then I saw Mozart walking slowly first through the kitchen and then out to the porch. At the door he sat down blinking in the bright light. He put his head down for a moment, then sat, sphinx-like staring out.

No bat floated out of the house, and I began to feel a bit foolish. I walked toward the house. Mozart stood up and gave me his usual effusive greeting. He stretched each back leg in turn, and then arched his back as he rubbed the side of his face against the doorjamb, purring with pleasure. Beside him lay the lifeless form of the bat.

This was not my first bat experience at Highland Farm. Soon after the first two donkeys came to the farm, I was cleaning the barn early one morning when I saw a bat swooping around the large water trough. As it flew it made its electric buzzing sounds but did not seem to be in good control, landing on the floor and hopping a few steps before flying off again. My immediate thought was that it was rabid and that the vet would want to test it. If this one were rabid, then others in the colony could be as well. And local residents might need to be warned. I went to the house to get an empty coffee can, and with equal amounts of courage and fear, I managed to scoop the bat into the can and quickly secured the lid. I drove to the vet's office. I had only met Brian once when he had come to see the donkeys the day they arrived. He had, I think, been surprised that with an extended pasture and a large barn that would easily hold a herd of cows, I should choose to adopt two small, old donkeys. However, Brian is a jolly soul and had genuinely wished me good luck.

Now I was in the waiting room of his surgery, explaining my mission to his assistant, Sheila. She listened carefully and disappeared into the back room. She came back quite quickly and said, "Brian says we don't do bats. But we will get rid of it for you if you like."

"No, that's all right," I said a little startled and left clutching the coffee can which was still emitting those strange electric clickings.

How little I knew! I later learned that bats come under medical scrutiny only when they have bitten someone and the test can only be done in specially equipped labs and only locally in select places like the University of New Hampshire or Cornell.

There I was driving along Route 11 in my little red pickup truck with an almost assuredly rabid bat making strange noises in a coffee can on the seat beside me. What would I say if I were stopped for speeding? I slowed down. What if I got in an accident and the lid came off? Surely the bat would fly out and bite me. I wished I had left it at the vet's office. How could I get rid of it safely? Around the next corner I saw a Dairy Queen in the distance. They must have a dumpster, I thought. It was too early for anyone to be there. No one would see me. There was nobody in sight as I drove up beside the huge trash container. I let the coffee can roll down the inside edge so it would land softly on trash already there.

It was many months before I stopped to buy an ice cream. I think I expected to hear sounds of an angry rabid bat still echoing through the dumpster.

We have not had another bat in the house, but there are always plenty in the barn in the summer. Each August for some reason there are frequently dead baby bats on the barn floor in the morning. One day I found nine. I don't know why they die. I'm careful not to touch them but have looked at them closely, and they are perfect in every detail: tiny teeth delicate nostrils, translucent ears, and filigree feet. And like all of nature's miniatures, totally vulnerable.

◆   ◆   ◆

Mozart is a city cat. I am not sure he will ever feel comfortable living in the country with its rough terrain and large animals. A Labrador on a leash was the largest animal he had ever encountered before coming to New Hampshire. During the first spring at the farm he moved cautiously, belly low to the ground as he explored his new surroundings. So when I saw him tear flat out across the front lawn, I knew something new to him would follow. A few feet behind and probably unaware of Mozart, was a bull. He was magnificent. He walked sedately over the lawn. The sun shone on his rippling brown back, and he tossed his head from side to side, snorting and exhilarating in his newfound freedom.

As a very young child on that farm in Surrey, I watched a bull that had arrived that day from a neighboring farm. He was in a small enclosure near the milking barn where he could walk about. I knew that Jersey bulls were smaller than the cows and that they were extremely ferocious. This bull was sleeping in the sun; his hindquarters were back against the fence where I was standing.

I was fascinated by how smooth his coat looked particularly on the inside of his upper hind legs, and I reached through the fence to see if the sack between his legs felt as velvety as it looked. In one gigantic leap the bull was at the other end of the enclosure. He faced me head down. Breathing hard he pawed the ground, the sun flashing on the ring in his nose. The farmer came running out of the milk barn, picked me up, and, back in the barn, dropped me unceremoniously to the floor.

Now I saw Mozart crouched under the truck, hackles raised and bushy tailed. I dialed the farmer's number. Yes, he'd get some help and be right over. I went outside to see where the bull had gone so I could tell the farmer when he came. The bull was down by the lower level of the barn in a corner with fencing on two sides of him. I talked to him as he ate the tall grass. He seemed quite content, and I moved closer. He seemed smaller than when he had suddenly appeared on the lawn. Standing there quietly chewing, he reminded me of Ferdinand, that gentle bull who liked to sit under the cork trees and smell the flowers. I found myself stroking his neck while I talked to him, and he really liked it when I scratched behind his ears.

That is how we were when Roger, the farmer, and his two strong friends arrived carrying ropes and a chain.

"You better leave him be," said Roger, "he ain't goin' to like us so good."

"Jeezum Crow," said the older man, "ain't you afeard o' nothin? That ain't no cow."

It took the men a while to lead the bull into the trailer. As he lunged and cavorted, resisting their efforts to load him, he seemed even larger than when I first saw him walking so proudly across the lawn.

Finally, I heard the heavy door slam shut, and the trailer disappeared down the hill. Only then did I try to urge Mozart out from under my truck. As I walked across the lawn holding Mozart, I was glad that this time I had chosen the right end of the bull.

5

HANNA, ANNIE, AND EMMA

The advertisement read: "Three-month-old brown donkey, female. Needs lots of TLC. $50 (and the phone number)." I called.

It turned out that the young donkey had gotten tangled in some barbed wire and in her panic to get free had torn her hind legs badly. Then they became infected. Now they were healed, but the poor little donkey needed to be somewhere else so that she could recover from the pain and trauma of daily medical treatments. I said I would come and pick her up that weekend.

Borrowing a trailer from a nearby farmer, I set off for Connecticut. I was anxious to help this little donkey begin a better life. She would be my first brown donkey. Being brown meant that her antecedents had come from Spain. It was George Washington who first imported donkeys to this country. They are not indigenous. He imported a number of Spain's tall brown donkeys in order to have strong working mules for his army. General Washington permitted only his most purebred mares to breed with these donkeys to produce the treasured mules.

After three hours heading south on Route 395, I turned onto a narrow country road and from there into a small pleasant farm with chickens and three brown donkeys. Hanna, the small one I had come to collect, was standing next to her older sister Sunny. The other donkey was their mother, Annie.

Hanna was so small and so frightened that I worried about her being alone in the trailer for three hours. Cautiously, I asked if Annie might also be for sale. "Actually, you can have her if you like," was the answer. Annie walked calmly up the ramp into the trailer with Hanna right beside her. I drove north.

Harriet was at home when I arrived that evening. She peeked in the trailer. "Mom, there are two donkeys in there; what's up?" I told her the story as she led Annie to the small pasture with Hanna trotting at her side. We watched as they rolled in the grass.

Brian checked them over the next morning. He thought that Hanna's legs had finally healed, though he shook his head at what the original wounds must have been. He said that in time the deep scars might be covered by fur. "Yes, she will need a lot of gentle care," he said as he tried to calm the struggling little donkey. Then he looked Annie over carefully. Seeing her through his eyes, I could tell from her swayed back and knobby knees that she was pretty old. He looked at her teeth and said "This old girl is healthy, and she is forty if she is a day. Lots of chickens at that place," he added. It was not a question.

"How did you know?" I asked.

"Lice," he said. "They are very common where you have chickens." Brian said he had a spray that would clear up the lice. We were to keep these two separate from the other donkeys for a week, and we were not to touch them for two days. Harriet followed Brian back to the clinic to get the spray, and while they were there, Brian showed her a louse under the microscope. She was still wide-eyed when she returned. "So gross!" she said. "If you magnified it a thousand times it would be scarier than any monster you could imagine."

When the quarantine was over, Annie and little Hanna joined the other donkeys in the big pasture. Old Annie walked calmly into their midst and instantly became the matriarch of the herd. Dark chocolate brown and taller by several hands than the smaller gray ones around her, Annie was always easy to see at the center of the group. For the next four years Annie lived out the remainder of her long life peacefully at Highland Farm.

Annie was completely gentle and companionable not only with other donkeys but also with people as well. On weekends when Harriet and Kate were home we would take mugs of coffee and go into the barn after dinner and talk sitting on the barn floor amongst the donkeys. Nahum and Solomon were frequently already lying down, and if I sat beside one of them, he would likely stretch his head across my lap. All the donkeys delighted in these nocturnal visits that might last several hours. Finding us sitting down rather than standing up was a novelty for the donkeys, and they took the opportunity to sniff our faces and hair, nibbling a bit here and there and even tried grooming us with their muzzles. They never stepped on us or were anything but gentle in their curiosity.

"Mom," Harriet whispered quietly as we sat on the barn floor one evening. I looked over to see Annie lapping coffee from Harriet's mug with her tongue. Sometimes Annie would follow me around while I worked in the field, or she would clatter off in her awkward old gait if the donkeys went on a tear. She was just sensible, kind old Annie who seemed openly to enjoy the last few years of her life.

Hanna grew tall and strong. The scars on her hind legs became faint and finally disappeared under her thick brown fur. It was not long before she wanted to be brushed along with the others and insisted on having her share of the carrots. When she felt comfortable enough to leave her mother's side, she bonded with Molly, a small gray donkey who was perpetually overweight. They made an odd couple in the pasture. Hanna was also devoted to Harriet's cat, Miss Pocket.

Miss Pocket came to stay at the farm when Harriet lived in a small apartment in Boston where she worked. Miss Pocket adapted quickly, and if she were not asleep on the couch beside Mozart, the resident cat, she could be found in the barn. She knew every corner of it and climbed the highest beams. In winter evenings while I got the barn ready for the donkeys to come in for the night, Miss Pocket sat on the partition watching, and I realized that she was waiting for Hanna. Out in the pasture Hanna followed Miss Pocket, and they would walk single file on narrow paths through the grass. Sometimes Miss Pocket curled up in the grass and slept; Hanna would lean down and sniff her gently with her muzzle. Miss Pocket had a favorite place to sit deep in a huge retaining wall of granite rocks beside the barn. The only way you could tell if she were in there was to look for her shining amber eyes. Hanna always knew when she was in there and would reach up to her with her muzzle.

Sometimes we took Hanna and Jenny with us for a walk in the woods. Hanna walked eagerly and seemed interested in the surroundings. Out in the pasture she would suddenly run very fast in tight circles, kicking up her hind legs in abandon. Often she ran on three legs. It was a comical sight, and we felt sure that she enjoyed our amusement. Remembering the shivering, terrified little creature that had arrived at the farm just a few months before, it was hard to believe she was the same animal.

One sunny afternoon the following April I rolled back the big door on the south side of the barn to let in the warm air. Looking up from my sweeping I saw that a car had parked at the edge of the road. A tall middle-aged woman was walking up the grassy slope. She introduced herself as Sheila Barrett, and she wondered if we might talk for a moment since she had a question to ask me. We sat on the screened porch from which we could see Mupo and the donkeys grazing on the hillside.

Sheila said she lived about five miles east of Highland Farm and had a number of chickens, two goats, a ferret, and a donkey. She had adopted the donkey from the Bureau of Land Management, which periodically rounds up some of the wild donkeys and mustangs in the Southwest and sends them to other parts of the country for adoption. Grasslands in parts of the Southwest are inhabited by roaming herds of these animals and can become overcrowded particularly in the eyes of the farmers when the donkeys stray onto private ranches. The ranchers have been known to shoot the trespassers on sight. Many hundreds of donkeys and mustangs have found excellent homes through this program that is monitored carefully. The adopter has to have a certain amount of pasture and pays a nominal fee. If the animal is sold, it may not be sold for more than the original price. The Bureau of Land Management reserves the right to follow up on adopted animals to make sure they are well treated.

Sheila had had her donkey, Emma, for two years. Al, the donkey who lived at Blackwater Farm nearby, had been part of that same shipment to central New Hampshire. Sheila said she enjoyed the sight of her donkey in the field with the goats and chickens, but since she spent four days a week in Philadelphia teaching economics at a college there, she had had little time to spend with Emma. Sheila went on to tell me that in six weeks she was to begin her sabbatical and with a friend was going to explore the country for a year. She continued, "It would make me very happy if you would accept Emma as a gift."

I never met a donkey I didn't like, and the idea of having a former wild one was intriguing. The next day I went to Sheila's house. She had already left for Philadelphia but had encouraged me to visit Emma who was in the field with the goats and chickens. She was tall and gray. Her muzzle was white. The black dorsal stripe was handsomely prominent. Emma had a beautiful head with long well proportioned ears. She was quite heavy but it seemed to me that with some vigorous exercise in the steep pasture at Highland Farm she would slim down quite quickly. Emma looked up as I approached the gate. Donkeys are innately curious and friendly, but Emma looked wary and walked away. I wondered how long it would take for me to gentle her. How long would it be before I could touch her?

Sheila made arrangements with Emile Shaw to deliver Emma to Highland Farm. I was to expect her at four o'clock on Thursday. Emile Shaw's passion was horses. He delivered mail on a rural route early each morning so by afternoon he could train and race trotting horses for other people.

On weekends he was frequently out of state racing. More often than not he won. Every three months Emile came to the farm to trim the donkeys' hooves. He was infinitely kind and patient with animals, and from seeing him deal gently with recalcitrant horses and donkeys, I knew him also to be the strongest man I ever met.

Just before four o'clock on Thursday I went to the main gate to the pasture beside the barn. The donkeys and Mupo drifted down the field, always interested to see what might be happening. Four-thirty came and went and so did five o'clock. Hoping nothing had happened, I could only continue to wait. Finally, close to five-thirty I heard Emile's truck labor up the hill, pulling the trailer behind. He pulled in close to the gate and jumped out of the cab. He was wet from head to foot. His hair was matted and even his tough blue jeans were dark with sweat. Emile was not smiling. "I've wrestled this animal for an hour and a half to get her in the trailer. I guess she knows who won." As he let down the back of the trailer he told me to open the gate when he brought her out and to shut it fast once she was inside. With Emile holding the lead line, the terrified donkey exploded out of the back of the trailer. She was shaking, and she too was drenched in sweat. Her eyes were wild with fear. I swung open the gate and the donkeys inside scattered. Emma lurched towards it, and with a swift movement Emile unclipped the line from her halter and she leaped into the field.

Emma had had no reason to gallop for more than two years so her gait was stiff as she fled up the pasture. She did not stop until she reached the back fence. Because Emma was awkward and overweight, Mupo and the donkeys had no trouble keeping pace with her. Emile leaned on the gate. Finally he did smile. "I know you will make friends with her," he said, "but it won't be today!" He climbed back into his truck and drove off down the hill.

I was glad it was spring and that the donkeys need not be in the barn at night. Except in winter they spent the nights on the east side of the barn where they have shelter, the warmth of the early morning sun and can wander around freely. Emma would not feel confined, and I hoped that by winter she would be acclimated enough so that being inside the barn with the doors closed against storms and the cold would not bother her.

I watched as Mupo and the donkeys inspected their new member. There were squeals and snorts. Emma did not want them to get close—snaking out her head in an off-putting gesture. She lay down and rolled. Because she was heavy she was not able to roll from side to side but had to get up and then lie down to roll on the other side, which she did in order to dry her coat on the grass. Mupo and the donkeys stood around and watched. Emma shook herself vigorously and began to nibble the grass tentatively, keeping her eyes on the others. Soon all the heads were down eating grass too. Several times that evening I saw the herd suddenly gallop off to a different part of the field, Emma following stiff-legged.

Early the next morning when I took the animals their hay, they were all standing in the sun, and Emma was in the midst of them. When she saw me, she moved off and watched me closely. I thought how foolish I had been to think that it was I who would tame this still wild animal. Mupo and the donkeys would be the ones who would let her know she was safe. When she understood that, then she could begin to accept me.

And that is what happened. Each day it seemed that Emma was less alarmed at my presence and my voice when I fed and brushed the others. Soon the fear left her eyes when I was near her. She also lost the extra weight and was able to roll over and back without having to get up in between. Her gait became fluid, and it was exciting to watch her transform into the tall graceful animal she became.

Emma watched as I brushed the others each day, and she became increasingly curious about it. Then came the day I had longed for. I was brushing Jenny and talking to her as I always did when I realized that Emma had moved and was standing right next to me. Moving slowly and talking to her, I put the brush on her flank. She cringed momentarily but stood quite still while I brushed her side gently. I was careful not to let my hand touch her. Several days later I did rest my hand on her shoulder. She quivered, but did not move away, and she never minded again. Soon she let me brush both her face and her ears.

About six weeks after Emma came to the farm I was reminded of just how wild she had once been and probably would always remain to some extent. I had gone to the village for some errands and as I drove back to the top of the hill by the barn I saw Jenny standing in the middle of the road. Everywhere I looked it seemed there were donkeys: on the lawn, across the road, in my neighbor's vegetable garden, in the adjacent field.

Each spring it had become a ritual for the donkeys to either find or make a weak place in the fence and push through cavorting and kicking up their heels, snorting with delight. They always came back willingly when I enticed them with the sound of grain shaking in a coffee can. When I got them back in the barn, I sprinkled the grain on the floor for them to eat, piece by piece.

One year I was away on the day of their annual adventure and all the donkeys headed down the hill to the village where surprised, kind people caught them and brought them back to the farm. It happened to be Good Friday so the rescuers good-naturedly agreed that the donkeys were on their way to church. That escapade was duly reported with photographs in the local paper.

This time I was concerned because Emma was out, and I had no idea how I could coax her back if she were separated from the rest. I put grain in the can and shook it, calling the donkeys. They came across the road, around the house and up the lawn. I sprinkled grain on the barn floor intending to close the door when they were all in. They were all there but Emma, who was standing on the other side of the road. She was agitated, throwing her head up and down anxious at being separated from the herd.

She would not cross the road. It must have been that when they got out they all crossed the road together in a bunch, and Emma had not noticed the surface. Now she saw the stretch of black tarmac as a threat—perhaps as deep water or as a crevasse that might open into a canyon. I did the only thing I could think of. Leading old Annie out of the barn by her chin, we stood in the middle of the road. Annie kept chewing her mouthful of grain. Emma could see that we were neither swept away by rushing water, nor did we disappear into the bowels of the earth. Gingerly, she stepped onto the tarmac and with quick light steps she seemed to tiptoe across. Once over she bolted into the barn to join her companions.

It was not long before Emma became affectionate. She liked having her head rubbed as she leaned it against my chest. She objected only slightly when Emile trimmed her hooves or when Brian checked her over each spring. During winter she came up into the barn for the night with no hesitation. I think she liked the security of being part of a herd once again.

Emma's wildness never left her completely. Any sudden noise startled her, and she would trot in bouncing small steps, making a trumpeting sound through her nostrils that was clearly an alert, her eyes wary and fearful. At those times I knew not to touch her but to try to reassure her with my voice. All the donkeys were quick to notice any intruder to their pasture such as a fox or deer, but Emma was quicker. Sometimes she saw or sensed intruders beyond my vision. There might have been a moose or a coyote in the woods beyond. I'll never know but she did. At those times in particular I could see the stark, stunning wildness return to her.

Emma grew to be a handsome creature with her beautiful head and graceful body. It would have been exciting to breed her and to have her foal. But for that to happen she would have had to visit Al at Blackwater Farm, and I knew I could not inflict even that short trip on her. Nor could I ever ask Emile to load her into his trailer again!

6

SOME WILD, SOME NOT

One of the things that I really looked forward to when we moved to Highland Farm was the opportunity to see animals that lived wild in this remote and beautiful part of the country. I knew that there were beaver, otter, muskrat and mink that lived down the hill by Highland Lake, and wandering through the dense wood on the farm and stretching for miles beyond its borders were deer, moose, fox, bobcat, and coyote as well as raccoons. And from time to time bear were seen.

Many years before we came to the farm there had been a bear ranging through the area that was perceived as a threat. He came very close to houses in the village, and he may have killed a dog or some livestock and was considered potentially dangerous. Four men from the village met up at the farm with their guns in the hope of tracking him down. They stood under the sickle pear tree devising a plan. One of the men heard a noise and looked up. It was the bear, sitting comfortably on a branch eating the ripe, delicious fruit. His fur, old and dried out, was still in the barn when we arrived. Several years after we moved in, we were driving up the hill to the farm and two bear cubs scuttled across the road in front of the car. I wanted to get out and see where they went, but Herb said it could be dangerous as the mother might appear and be protective of her cubs. Those were the only bears we saw. But there were signs that bears lived in the woods: deep scratches in the trunks of trees, stumps of trees torn apart where they had looked for insects, and very rarely a sudden, strong smell of urine.

Our first wild animals were not so large, nor so dramatic. One of the first nights we were at the farm I was awoken by the sound of mice, many mice brazenly scuttling, dancing above us on the floor of the attic. Herb slept on peacefully, and surprisingly the sound did not wake Mozart who was asleep at the foot of the bed. I spoke to him indignantly, but he only raised his head for a moment and then went back to sleep. He may have known the attic was unheated and very cold. It was December. But next morning I put him on the attic stairs and closed the door behind him. Several hours later I opened it. He was sitting where I had left him. I don't know if he ever went up and prowled around, but his presence and feline odor must have been enough. We never heard mice again.

December twelfth was Herb's birthday. As we got dressed that morning I looked out to see Mozart sitting by the garage in the sun. Suddenly his hackles rose, and his eyes seemed very large. Following his gaze I saw two deer, both does, walking across the meadow to the vegetable garden. At this time of year it offered not much more than some Brussels sprouts and several ragged cabbages. But the deer were grateful. Herb and I watched in delight feeling that they had come to offer a special birthday greeting.

Shortly after the New Year, Herb flew to Australia to visit his older daughter. It was bleak and lonely after he left. The cold outside was biting. There were no animals in the barn yet. I didn't see the deer again, and the only animal to appear was a feral cat that came at odd times and seemed more like a fleeting shadow than a flesh-and-blood creature. I couldn't encourage him to stay because Mozart would have challenged him, and it would have been an ugly fight. In those first weeks Mozart preferred to stay indoors, mostly by the fire, and was content to explore the interior of his new domain. At night he slept curled up beside me under the covers.

In the middle of January, I drove to Brunswick, Maine, to pick up Harriet and her two roommates. They had just finished their mid-year exams, and all three were recovering from a prevalent stomach bug. When they came down to the living room the following morning close to noon, they were still in their pajamas and wrapped in down puffs. Curled up on the couches by the open fire, they said what they really wanted was chicken noodle soup or consommé. I had neither in the house. But having sat in the car most of the previous day, I welcomed the thought of walking down the steep hill to the village and its only small store.

It was a gray day and bitterly cold. The watery sun when it did appear gave no warmth at all. It was as silent as only winter can be. I walked down the snow-packed road; no cars came up, and none came down. Just before crossing the road to the village, there is the only outlet from Highland Lake. It is a low waterfall that drops into an open pool before turning into a narrow stream running under the road and through a field. Such thick ice covered the lake that pickup trucks could drive on it to get to the small ice-fishing huts that dotted the lake's surface.

As I approached the outlet, I heard a plop into the water. Before whatever had made the sound came back up, I moved quickly so I could see the edge of the ice and the pool below. It wasn't very long before an otter emerged from the pool carrying something in his mouth. He scrambled up onto the edge of the ice and, completely unaware of me, crouched over a freshwater clam which he ate. Leaving the empty shells on the ice, he dropped back into the pool. This was what I had hoped for, the opportunity to watch a wild animal go about his business without my being seen. I stood in fascination as back and forth he went for his food. Finally, my feet were so cold I had to move on. After he had dropped into the water once more, I moved quickly so that I did not disturb the rhythm of his routine. As I did, a mink scuttled from under a vacant dwelling and disappeared under an overturned rowboat beside the ice, not six feet from me.

Finally, with several cans of soup in my knapsack, I trudged up the hill, eager to tell the girls of my wildlife adventures. All three were fast asleep on the couches, and Mozart was curled up on the floor in front of the fire. The wood I had heaped on was ancient pruning from the apple orchard. What I did not know at the time was that burning apple-wood is highly soporific. So no wonder they were asleep. After the bitter cold of my trek and the warmth of the room, the sweet smell of the smoke seduced me too, and I curled up and slept.

Although I had never seen wild mink, I had seen mink. Several years before, when I was hiking in the northern most reaches of Iceland, I had steeled myself to visit a mink farm. Mink farming is a big industry in Iceland, and pelts are sent to Scandinavia and to Russia. The farm was sickening. There were rows and rows of small wire cages. Each held only one mink so it could not fight and scar the future pelt of another. The animals were sleek and had thick shiny coats from their diet of fish skin and walrus, both full of fat to make their fur resplendent. As I walked between the long rows of cages trying not to be ill, I could only be shamed by their reaction to me. Without exception they crouched as far back as they could in their cages, their faces set in a seething, snarling hostility.

I longed to fling open all the cages and open the doors to the building. But instead I left in tears. Some months later I read in the paper that one night several people had forced their way in and had freed all the mink. Who knows what their future held in the wild, but at least it was their own.

A year or so after we moved to Highland Farm, I walked down the hill to the lake just at dawn, because I wanted to see the early morning sun reflected on it. As I approached the water's edge, I saw a mink busily dismembering a crustacean. I was about four feet from him when he turned and saw me. There again was the ferocious, seething hostility, this time poised to strike. Though he was only the size of my foot, I felt vulnerable and, as the intruder, backed off quite shaken by his ferocity. Walking back through the trees I wondered if mink might have an inherited memory of their systematic slaughter through centuries that still alerted them to the horror of humans.

How different from the mink was the coyote that I also met by chance. Late one summer evening I went to pick blackberries in a remote section of the orchard. Blackberry bushes grew there in abundance. Sitting on the ground with a bowl on my lap, I picked berries lost in thought. With no sound to warn me, I found myself face to face with a coyote. Our heads were level and if either of us had leaned forward, we would have touched noses. His eyes held my gaze as if in interest. They were kind eyes, and I felt no fear of this animal that could have dispatched me with several well-placed bites. Involuntarily I whispered, "You are very beautiful." The coyote continued to hold my gaze. Suddenly he was gone. I didn't even see him turn.

Other coyote sightings were less benign. Several days after I brought three lambs to the farm I saw two coyotes sitting under a tree half way up the big pasture watching the lambs while they were cavorting in the small pasture by the house. They could not have squeezed through the gate nor could they have climbed the wire fence, but their silent scrutiny was ominous. After a while I put the lambs in the barn, and the coyotes left. I did not see them again, except on the day Harriet's mare Phoeba had her foal. When I slid back the big barn door to let in the sun, there he sat brazenly waiting, not twenty feet from the barn. When I screamed at him, he slunk off reluctantly, but he did not give up easily. I buried the afterbirth that afternoon and covered it with lime. The next morning it had been dug up and dragged across the grass.

Other wild animals made fleeting appearances. The one I least expected was the handsome bobcat that suddenly appeared at the top of the pasture one morning. He was so preoccupied with his prey, a small rodent, a squirrel perhaps, that I had plenty of time to watch him through binoculars. Then as suddenly as he had appeared, he was gone.

It was not unusual to see a red fox cross the pasture with his bushy tail straight out behind him. What intrigued me most about foxes was how task-oriented they are. They travel in a straight line right across the nine-acre pasture, never deviating to the left or the right. In winter and the snow, the large pasture had fox tracks across it as if laid out with a ruler. Fortunately, I never saw a fisher. In New Hampshire they are called fisher-cats. Larger than a marten and smaller than a wolverine, they are fiercely ferocious and kill small animals, including cats and even small dogs, and they are one of the few predators that eat porcupines.

Walking in the woods behind the pasture always brought the hope of seeing deer. But often that hope was lost by suddenly hearing Mozart's voice nearby. Unbeknownst, he would follow me, and then our walk turned into an exercise in bucolic sonar! Mozart must have had a Siamese gene or two, for his voice was unexpectedly loud and hollow. Nearby he would yowl, I would return his yowl, and in this way we kept track of each other through extended hikes in the woods. Gone, however, was the possibility of seeing any wildlife that must have thought Moz and I were visitors from outer space. We returned from these walks with Mozart draped around my neck like a scarf and me holding his front and back paws for balance. He was a marvelous cat!

One morning when we were having breakfast on the porch, we noticed one of the donkeys eating amongst the tall rushes by the pond. You could only see its back. Then I realized we didn't have a donkey that color brown. Just then it raised its head and became a deer. It is so exciting to see deer; they are so beautiful and regal in their bearing. She looked about her, then a fawn stood up beside her, and together they walked through the orchard to the thick woods beyond. The fawn with its speckled back looked a little unsteady, and we wondered if it had been born in the rushes during the night.

Often in late fall, four or five deer dotted the northern part of the big pasture. Though they didn't mingle with the donkeys, they seemed quite comfortable with each other. Hunting season was the two-week period we really dreaded and hoped the deer would recede into the woods. Also, to a man with a gun who had had a couple of beers, grazing donkeys would surely look like easy targets, so I put them in the barn in the afternoon and kept them there until midmorning the next day to minimize the possibility of disaster. The farm was posted "No Hunting" quite clearly, and fortunately those signs were respected.

"For we like sheep," one of the familiar sections of Handel's "Messiah," is repeated several times by the chorus. As a child I thought it was a statement of affection, realizing only much later that "Have gone astray" was part of the same sentence. But we do like sheep. Dotted on a peaceful hillside they are picturesque. Lambs gamboling in the sun are the epitome of spring. From biblical times, sheep have symbolized meekness and vulnerability, and I wonder if over the centuries the meekness and vulnerability of domesticated sheep have left them helpless. Usually living in large groups and often herded by clever dogs, they have become virtually anonymous. Even the name sheep is the same singular and plural. How different are the ones we see from their wild counterparts who survive and breed on windswept moors and are the sentinels of distant hills. On sheep farms, lambing time means that farmers and vets work around the clock, helping in the birthing process to an extent that no other animal requires. Domesticated sheep have no tolerance for physical or emotional stress, and the extension of that is, as Brian the vet told me, "A sick sheep is a dead sheep." The sick sheep on our farm did die, but the stranger thing to me was that though I sat with her all through that day and night, she seemed to take no interest or comfort in my presence, my voice or my hands.

We had sheep at the farm for their wool and their meat. Thirty years ago, meat was still considered to be an important part of one's diet. Like homegrown fruit and vegetables, homegrown meat is so much better than the meat that is commercially available. We would get lambs in the spring that otherwise would go directly to market and keep them until fall. The poet, Jane Kenyon, and her husband Donald Hall, also a poet, were guests at dinner one evening, and Jane said how delicious everything tasted. Jane was a tender and fragile person. Somewhat hesitantly, I said that everything on our plates, lamb, new potatoes, and green beans had all been grown on the farm. There was a pause; then she said quietly, "fruits of the earth."

The first year there were three sheep: Shadrach, Meshach, and Abednego. The following year we had Winken, Blinken, and Nod. The last year we had sheep there were five: Matthew, Mark, Luke, And, as well as John. And was a handsome black sheep. No matter where they went, into the barn or out or just wandering in the field, they always walked in single file, solemn like small Anglican bishops. I like to think that their lives, short though they were, were good; a safe harbor in the barn at night, good grain twice a day, clean water, and a lovely pasture in which to spend their days.

When the lambs first arrived, they huddled in the corner of the pasture bleating and pathetic. It took many frustrating days to get them to follow me into the barn at night and out into the pasture in the morning. Often I gritted my teeth mumbling "for we like sheep." They stopped hurtling around in panic when they finally learned that I had grain, and like the children in the forest dropping pebbles so they could get home, I dropped grain at brief intervals to lure the sheep in and out of the barn. Finally after many days of this they caught on. Then understanding that I was the food-and-care person, they followed me everywhere. The little lamb, with fleece as white as snow, that followed Mary everywhere must have known that she had grain in the pocket of her sweet little dress!

Taking sheep to be slaughtered was no pleasure but part of growing one's food. It would have been easy to hire someone to take them away and so avoid the inevitable sadness, but that seemed less than honest. A week or so after I took them, one by one in the back of the station wagon, I went back to pick up neatly wrapped, flash-frozen packages in brown paper bags. Some went to our freezer, and the rest to relatives and friends who bought them. Several months later the beautiful soft white shearlings arrived that bore no resemblance to the dense, oily and slightly dirty coats that had kept the sheep warm and dry.

One trip to the butcher was memorable. Harriet was with me, and one of the sheep was standing meekly behind us in the station wagon. So there were three heads in a row: the sheep's, Harriet's, and mine. A small boy peered at us out of the rear window of the car in front. Then he turned and gesticulated to his parents in the front seat, obviously telling them that there was a sheep in the car behind. You can imagine the response. "No, dear, sheep don't ride in cars." More wild gesticulations and jumping around. So, to redeem the child, smiling and waving, we passed the other car. In the rear view mirror we could see two startled faces.

As I write this, I wonder about the difference between the mink and the sheep. It is easy to say that our sheep had good lives. Yes, they did. Although most of us now eat meat only rarely, for many people it is an important source of food. Perhaps the difference is those terrible cages and the fact that no one but an Eskimo needs fur.

7

THE SECOND GENERATION

Word about the donkey farm spread, so I was not surprised when late one Sunday the phone rang.

"You the donkey lady? You want another jackass?"

The old farmer on the other end of the line told me that he had that day bought two longhorn cattle and to close the deal he had had to take a donkey that lived with them as well. Mincing no words he said he had no use for the donkey but would be kind enough to let me have her for one hundred dollars.

The next day I drove to the farm where in a small barn a donkey was tied to a manger between two cattle. She seemed nervous as she tried to keep out of the way of those long horns. The donkey was bigger than my small Mediterranean ones. She was big enough for me to ride. I ran my hands over her back and down her legs as she eagerly ate her hay. She did not seem to mind my touch. I asked if I might brush her. It was late spring, molting time, and her unkempt coat came out in handfuls. Leaning in to me as I brushed, she seemed to be giving me her trust. I liked her. The old farmer watched, "Don't know nothin' about her, but she'll clean up pretty good I guess."

Early that evening a rickety old truck with the donkey peering over the top labored up the steep hill to the farm. The truck pulled in by the gate to the pasture where I was waiting with the eight donkeys. They sensed something was about to happen.

The old man unloaded the eager donkey. I gave him five twenty-dollar bills and led her to the gate. Through the gate the donkeys sniffed noses with the newcomer for a moment. That is the standard equine greeting, nostril to nostril. When I opened the gate and took off her halter, she kicked up her heels and galloped off up the pasture with the smaller donkeys keeping up as best they could.

"What do you do with all them critters?" he asked.

"Nothing," I replied., "I just like them."

"Now I've seen everything," he muttered as he got back in his truck and drove off.

Later, Brian came to check the new donkey and give her the necessary shots. By now Brian was always curious to see new additions to the herd. He pronounced her healthy and about five years old. We sat on the steps at the back of the barn watching the donkeys graze in the late evening sun. "This has got to be donkey heaven," he said.

At this time of year all the donkeys had shed their heavy winter coats and were sleek and shiny. But no matter how much I brushed the new one, she kept the thick soft white fur on her belly and on her forehead. So the name, Shaggs, seemed to fit.

The provenance of donkeys is often obscure. I knew nothing of Shaggs prior to her overnight stay in the barn across the valley. I had no idea if she had been ridden or used for farm work or if she had originally been one of the wild ones brought from the Southwest. But I didn't think she had been a wild one because she came up into the barn using the curved ramp under it and did not mind when the door was shut behind her. A recently wild one would have. Also she did not mind being tied to a rail while I checked her hooves. I felt she had grown up around people. A few days after she came, and when she was out in the pasture with the other donkeys, I leaned my weight over her back ready to step away quickly if she objected. She went on eating. Finally, I swung my leg over her back and sat squarely on her. She went on eating, so I stayed there for quite a while enjoying the day with the donkeys.

Walking in the woods was a pleasant outing, and we often took Shaggs with us, but she would only go if another donkey went as well, preferably Jenny to whom she had become attached. Sometimes I rode Shaggs, and Herb led Jenny or we walked between them.

Ever since Jenny's false pregnancy, I had longed to have one of the donkeys give birth at the farm. When Shaggs came in heat she went to spend a week or so with Al at Blackwater Farm, about three miles away. Al was a handsome donkey who had been wild in the Southwest and like so many others, had been brought north and adopted. Al had only sheep, chickens, and geese for company and was excited to see Shaggs. He had had two previous visitors from the farm. Neither had conceived.

But Shaggs did. As the thirteen-month gestation period came to a close, I worried about putting her in a stall by herself. She was always in the middle of the herd, never off by herself. I hoped I'd realize when the birth was imminent, and then I could put her in a stall so she could look after the foal when it arrived.

Several days later when we were sitting in the living room, talking to a friend after dinner, we heard a raucous heehaw. "It's Shaggs," I said. "She's had her foal." We ran out to the field in the dark and there she stood dazed with a small bundle of wet fur at her feet. The other donkeys were standing near her. Our friend led Shaggs to the waiting stall in the barn, and I picked up the small, wet foal and followed. In the quiet of the barn we gave Shaggs some grain and told her how wonderful she was, but she was not the least interested in her foal. I helped it stand on its long, thin legs and helped it find the milk. Finding it, the foal nursed hungrily. But Shaggs was impatient and kept moving away, not wanting to be bothered.

We let the other donkeys in to the main part of the barn in the hopes that Shaggs, feeling her friends close by, would relax and take care of her foal. As the donkeys came up into the barn, I turned and saw Shaggs leap over the four-foot door of her stall and trot toward her friends. Right behind her, not an hour old, the little wet foal, still streaked with blood, clambered over the same door and followed her mother with wobbly steps.

Quite by coincidence another donkey was born at the farm two days after Shaggs had hers. Several months prior, we had been given a very small Mediterranean donkey whose name was Sweet Pea. She was good-natured and perfect for a small child to ride. So when I heard of a family in the eastern part of New Hampshire who was looking for a donkey for their five-year-old daughter, I called. From our telephone conversation it was clear that the family had an extensive farm with horses and llamas and several large donkeys. They said they would be happy to trade Sweet Pea for one of their donkeys.

My daughter Harriet was home that weekend, and we drove east toward the coast. It was a pleasant, well-cared-for farm. Each year the owners went to the auction of exotic animals in Missouri, and this year had returned with two llamas, several spotted donkeys, one, brown and white that I liked very much. While we were talking, leaning on the fence, out of the barn walked a tall gray donkey. Yet he was not pure donkey. He had black stripes on his body and legs. He was a zedonk, half donkey and half zebra, which is rare, and it turned out that he had the docile donkey personality rather than the unpredictable, often difficult, zebra personality. The zedonk walked over to us and invited affection. He had a gentleness that was most appealing. Harriet liked him, and we both really wanted him. He would have been an elegant addition to the herd. But no, they would not part with him.

Susie, the spotted brown donkey, came home with us that day in the trailer. Susie was tall, big-boned and with large cinnamon-colored patches on her white coat. She had gentle brown eyes and adapted instantly to the other donkeys and life at the farm. When Brian came, he said she was healthy and perhaps twelve years old. He could tell she had had several foals from the number of small tears on her vagina. He said she was in foal again. As the weeks went by it was hard to know who would deliver first, Shaggs or Susie.

When Shaggs delivered first and was so disinterested in her foal, I put them in the small pasture with the five sheep and added Susie for company. Susie was huge and when drops of milk began to show on her teats, I put her in a stall by herself. She seemed calm but she tried to nip my hand when I tried to brush her flanks. Late that night when I went out to the barn for my nightly check of the animals before going to bed, Susie had delivered. He was just like her, brown and white but with blue and white eyes. Susie had cleaned him though he was still wet, and he was suckling happily. The rest of the donkeys across the barn knew what had happened and made quiet noises of excitement as they looked toward Susie's stall. Earlier that evening we had been listening to some Bach. So Sebastian became his name.

Young female donkeys are not at risk for harm by other members of the herd, and so Shaggs's foal Polly, as she was called, became a member of the herd right away and was looked after by other female members, only going to her mother to nurse. Young males, however, are at risk from other males who are known to attack and kill them. It is their way of reducing potential competition. Nicholas Nye, one of the three males, had been gelded when he was young and was now about eight years old. Susie seemed anxious to be back in the big pasture with the other donkeys, and after ten days Sebastian seemed strong enough and would make a good companion for Polly. Also he was beginning to nip and to chase the sheep.

I opened the big door of the barn and let Susie and Sebastian out. Susie went off to graze. Sebastian started to follow her. Immediately Nicholas Nye bellowed and lunged at Sebastian, his neck snaked out, his teeth bared. Luckily I was close enough to run between them yelling. Nicholas

Nye was so startled he veered off snorting. I grabbed Sebastian and pulled him into the barn; Susie was right behind me. Still shaking, I led them back to the small pasture where they spent the next weeks until Sebastian was big and strong and quite able to protect himself. When next I put them in the big field with the others, Nicholas Nye ignored him.

Polly and Sebastian quickly became friends. They groomed each other with their teeth and playfully chased each other in an impromptu race across the field, which was heightened by playful nips. Although they were the same height at birth, Sebastian quickly overtook Polly in size. As in other species, the male donkey develops more quickly than the female. By the time he was seven months old, Sebastian was tall and very beautiful. He had kept his blue and white eyes giving him a rakish look. Soon he began to behave as if he were the dominant male, which, I realized, he was. The other donkeys had little patience when Sebastian tried to herd them to another part of the field or get them up when they were lying down napping in the sun. He bullied Nicholas Nye. Then he started bothering the females, asserting his rights over them. The peaceful dynamics of the herd had disappeared, and Polly was much too young to be bred. I had to make a choice. Either find another home for Sebastian or have him gelded. I couldn't do that. He was an extraordinary example of his species, and I felt he should have the opportunity to be part of its continuation.

It was not difficult to find him another home where he would have his own herd of females and fulfill his role as dominant male. But it was sad to see that handsome animal leave as he bounced into the trailer that was to take him to his new home in Vermont. But I was grateful for the peace that immediately returned to the herd.

One Sunday shortly after Sebastian's departure I received a call from a neighbor across the valley. Ann raised a special breed of sheep known for the high quality of their wool. She sheared them herself and spun the soft wool into yarn and then sold it for considerable sums. Ann began to cry as she told me what had happened that morning. She and her husband had

had breakfast in the kitchen as they always did so they could watch her beloved sheep grazing in the field right next to the house. Then they went upstairs to change for church. Just minutes later when they came down twelve of the sheep lay dead, mauled and eviscerated by two blood-spattered coyotes on a killing spree, who were at that moment closing in on two other sheep while the remaining ones ran bleating in every direction. Ann and her husband had run out screaming, and the coyotes left, looking over their shoulders as they trotted away. Instead of going to church that morning Ann and her husband dug a deep grave for the defenseless creatures that had been so wantonly slaughtered.

The reason Ann said she was calling was that she had heard that in other parts of the country donkeys were used as guards for sheep, and she wondered if that were true. We talked for quite a while, and I told her what I knew which was yes, donkeys make excellent sheep guards for two reasons. The first is that any canine is the natural enemy of a donkey. If a canine gets close, the donkey will bite the back of its neck holding it while the sharp front hooves break its back. Poodle, retriever, or coyote, the donkey makes no distinction. The deadly injury is quickly inflicted.

The other reason that donkeys are good sheep guards is that they eat the same food as sheep, grass in summer, hay in winter, and drink clean water. Dogs, especially in Europe, are used as sheep guards, but they require separate feeding and care.

The donkey that guards sheep cannot be just any donkey as I once thought—with disastrous results. I had given Willi, a male donkey, to a friend to guard some sheep, but the donkey had mistaken two male baby lambs for baby male donkeys and had summarily killed them. The sheep-guard donkey has to be a young female who has not had a foal. She would therefore feel protective of the sheep. Also, the donkey could no longer be treated as a pet but rather as a working animal always with her charges and always on duty. There was a long pause at the other end of the line, and

Ann asked me if I had such a donkey. There was another long pause while I realized that I did.

The next morning I put Polly's halter and lead line on, and we started our three-mile walk. On the other side of the fence, the remaining donkeys followed us as far as the field would let them. Even Shaggs was as agitated as the others in their concern for what was clearly the departure of the young donkey. Polly seemed oblivious of the other donkeys, her small hooves prancing enthusiastically as we started down the steep hill to her new home. A mile down the road, we crossed the brook by Highland Lake and went by the houses in the village. Then we went over the trestle bridge and across Route 11, up the hill by the white church and the small elementary school, down another steep, winding road by Hale Shaw's dairy farm to Polly's new home.

Ann was waiting at the gate when we arrived. I gave Polly a hug, and in her long ear I whispered good wishes. Ann held the lead line, and she took her in the field where fourteen sheep were huddled together in a corner. Free of her halter, Polly trotted around the field checking its perimeters. In a gesture of comfort and ownership, she lay down and rolled, then began to nibble the grass.

I left knowing that I must not return for many months, until she had accepted the responsibility of guarding the sheep and no longer looked to me as her caregiver. A few days later Ann called and said Polly was fine. The sheep kept close to her all the time, and there had been no further sign of coyotes.

It was eighteen months later that I finally went to see Polly. No one was home. I walked to the gate. Now there were twenty-two sheep, and Polly, full-grown and filled-out, stood among them as they nibbled the grass. Polly lifted her head and looked at me. I did not say a word, but I know she recognized me. I saw it in her eyes. But now I was a stranger, and she moved off, taking her sheep with her. I was very proud.

8

NAHUM AND SOLOMON

For the past six years Nahum and Solomon have greeted the early light of day with a heehaw. Solomon's is first, an exuberant bray that rings out triumphant across the meadows and over the lake. As the sound fades, Nahum brays as if to reaffirm Solomon's statement. That is the way it has been for them—one following the other, totally inseparable for thirty-two years. Now they are gone. Nahum died on Tuesday and Solomon on Wednesday morning, and in the evening they were buried together. That was yesterday.

It has been brutally cold these past two months since the beginning of the New Year, and little or no snow has fallen. Frost was four feet into the ground, so when Mark Thompson came with his back hoe to bury the donkeys, he had to move the manure pile and dig the grave deep beneath it where the frost had not permeated.

Nahum and Solomon were the first two donkeys that came to the farm. They had been together all their lives and had been born at the Danby Farm in Nebraska, which was famous for breeding donkeys of stock imported from Italy. The donkeys had Italian names on their pedigree papers. Since everything was new to them, including my voice, we decided to change their names to honor two previous owners of Highland Farm. Nahum Batchelder ran for governor at the turn of the twentieth-century on the Grange ticket against the expansion of the railroad. He won, and once elected refused to go to the capitol, Concord. Instead he ran the state out of what is now our dining room.

Solomon was named for Herb's father who was a successful and benevolent businessman. Solomon Agoos bought the farm from Governor Batchelder in 1934 and retreated from Boston to its peace and quiet each weekend.

When the donkeys first arrived, they were shy and skittish. In the ell of the barn that had originally been a carriage house there is a small room that I set up for their loose box. Adjoining it is a larger room that leads directly out to their pasture and gave them shelter from rain, snow, and heat. Never did they soil the wood shavings where they slept, but did only in one corner of the larger room. Donkeys are like that. They are clean animals, and they also rely on ritual and routine. Nahum and Solomon quickly established times to be indoors and outdoors. They seemed to know when it was about to rain, coming in just ahead of the first drops.

The day they arrived I could not tell them apart and wondered if I ever would. During those first days in particular, I spent many hours with them in their pasture, sitting, watching, and talking to them so they would get used to my voice as well as my presence. Donkeys are insatiably curious. Hesitantly at first they approached me, sniffing and snorting tentatively. Their differences became apparent quickly. Nahum's ears were longer and bowed like parentheses. Solomon's were shorter and quite straight. Nahum's coat was lighter gray than Solomon's. Solomon's personality was eager, alert, demanding. If I brushed Nahum, Solomon would squeeze between us, and so I bought a second brush and stood between them as I groomed them at the same time.

After the fifth day of spending time with them in their new surroundings, I thought I would leave them alone for a change. I heard Solomon heehaw. It was a summons. Donkeys are naturally friendly, and I have found them to be openly affectionate to each other and to people. There was always a kindness about Nahum and a gentleness to an extent that I have seldom seen in a large animal. If I sat down on the floor of the barn beside where he was lying, he would put his head across my lap and close his eyes in bliss as I stroked his ears. Or if I took a mug of tea and sat on the barn floor with the donkeys in the evening, he would come over and rest his muzzle on my shoulder. His head became heavy as he became drowsy.

On a whim one day I called Mrs. Langfeld at Danby Farm in Nebraska and asked her about her farm. At any one time, she told me, there would be two hundred donkeys. She and her husband had bred them for many years. I had Nahum and Solomon's papers in my hand as I spoke and told her the names of their antecedents. Mrs. Langfeld remembered Nahum's father vividly. "Why he was the kindest donkey we ever had," she said. "Each jack had his herd of twenty jennies," she continued, "and we never had to separate him at foaling time the way we did with all the other jacks. He loved the little ones. He liked to baby-sit them and teach them how to groom each other; things like that. He was a sweetheart," she finished.

Nahum and Solomon did live longer than many donkeys, but it was their devotion to each other that was extraordinary. Grazing in the meadow they were always side-by-side close enough to touch. Even when there were as many as ten other donkeys, a mule, and two horses in the field, they were always next to each other. At night in the barn they slept back to back like bookends, but without the books. They were eager when we took them for walks along the trails through the woods or to visit a neighbor. I only needed to put a halter on Nahum, Solomon stayed right beside us often trying to go between Nahum and me. Even though they were the smallest donkeys, they were the undisputed leaders of the herd for a year until Mupo came. But until she did, they were the first into the barn at night and first out the door in the morning. They also protected the herd and watched over them. On more than one occasion I saw Nahum and Solomon chase a fox out of the field, and woe betide any dog who came near, or for that matter any cat, goat, or sheep who entered their field.

When Madeline and Molly came to the farm, it was Madeline's initial separation from her foal. After the first excitement of meeting the four resident donkeys cantering around and generally getting her bearings in the new surroundings, I saw her suddenly stop. She raised her head and brayed. She was calling, calling her baby. Instantly Nahum and Solomon answered her call, each with his own urgent bray. Immediately Madeline was encircled not only by Nahum and Solomon but also by Jenny, Nicholas, and Molly who trotted right over to her. I have to think that they were offering her comfort as they did on another occasion the following year.

Late one evening when I went as usual to check the animals before going to bed, I found Madeline lying on her side kicking and rolling and groaning. At once I knew she had colic. Colic is when a donkey or horse gets a concentration of gas in its intestines that will not move. As in humans, it is excruciatingly painful, and for a horse or donkey extremely dangerous, for in the effort to alleviate the pain by rolling, they can twist their intestines, and that can kill them.

There was no time to call Brian to come and inject a muscle-relaxing drug. The only thing I could do was to get Madeline on her feet and to keep her walking so that the pocket of gas would move down the intestinal tract and be expelled in the normal process. I put a halter on her, got her up and led her out to the field. I spoke to her with encouragement, focusing all my attention on her. She walked awkwardly, obviously in distress. Soon she started to move more easily, so I knew the cure was beginning to work. I also knew that it could be many hours before she would have complete relief, and I could not leave her until then. It was a warm summer night with both moon and stars shining, they seemed almost within reach. Their light cast strong shadows of the tall maple trees across the grass. I expected to see the other donkeys grazing peacefully in the moonlight, but I did not. A sound made me turn and there, strung out in single file right behind Madeline, walked the eight donkeys led by Solomon and Nahum. They walked silently, solemnly behind us as we circled the field again and again until the wee hours of the morning, loyal, gentle beasts trying to help.

The only time I saw Nahum and Solomon apart was the day Nahum followed me up the porch steps and into the house. Solomon and I were both surprised, and he waited outside while Nahum, always curious, walked around the kitchen, through the hall, and into the living room. I followed him, wondering if he would go upstairs the way my donkey in England had. He ignored the stairs and went into the dining room. He was perfectly at home and eager to look around. In the living room he jumped delicately from rug to rug. I think it was because the hardwood floors shine, and he decided that they might be wet. He returned to the kitchen, then out to the porch and jumped down to where Solomon was waiting nervously.

I separated them once when Nahum cut his leg, and I did not want Solomon butting against me as I cleaned it. Even though they could touch noses over the heavy fence, I thought they would either break it or hurt themselves because they banged so hard against it to be together. I never did that again.

Their relationship was one of calm companionship, but perhaps three times a year they played out an emotional ritual that was the same each time. Solomon would sniff and snort, his nostrils touching Nahum's. Then they both snorted and made provocative sounds of affection. This was followed by each trying to nip the other's front knees. It was a quest for dominance. When one was forced to kneel, if only briefly, the other put his head over the neck of the kneeling donkey. They repeated this pantomime of dominance five or six times. Sometimes it seemed that Solomon won, sometimes Nahum. The ritual ended with one mounting the other sideways. I think it was an enthusiastic display of friendship, like a hug.

It turns out that Solomon was well named. His early morning bray became known as the Song of Solomon. At other times when he brayed, the sound was also a song of greeting, of pleading, or of frustration. Solomon was the leader of the herd until Mupo, the beautiful mule, arrived. Then she became the dominant animal, and Solomon, far from being bothered at being deposed, adored Mupo following her like a shadow.

The day that Mupo died, I kept the other donkeys in the barn so that they would not be distressed. Mupo had been ill and was finally unable to walk. The only kind solution was to put her out of her misery and pain. Brian and his assistant came and laid down that vibrant, spirited animal under her favorite maple in the field she loved so well, and she was buried there immediately. Much later that evening I put the donkeys back into the field. Close to midnight I was awaken by the sound of heartbreak. Looking out our bedroom window I could see in the bright moonlight all the donkeys standing at Mupo's grave. On it stood Solomon, his head on one side braying on and on. It was the saddest requiem. The following morning Solomon resumed his leadership of the herd and retained it until he died.

Late this past autumn it was clear that this was to be Nahum and Solomon's final winter. They both suffered from arthritis and were losing weight. They looked gaunt. I wanted to be able to get them through this winter, hoping it would be a mild one, so that they could enjoy for one last time the warmth and bounty of spring. To help them through it, I gave each a small ration of grain every day for extra nourishment. Normally donkeys do not need grain on a regular basis. They do well on grass and hay. Historically they have been the beasts of burden of the poor, and for the poor grain is a staple and cannot be shared with a donkey.

Each day Nahum and Solomon ate their grain greedily and looked a little better. Everything was fine until the day before yesterday. In the afternoon Nahum was breathing hard and with a heavy discharge from his nostrils. Solomon stood close beside him. Brian came. "Damn," he said when he saw Nahum, "he guzzles his grain doesn't he?"

"Yes," I said wondering how he knew.

"He has got grain stuck in his esophagus, and it's beginning to block the trachea. Get me a bucket of lukewarm water." Brian went to his van and came back with a syringe and a thin rubber hose. He gave Nahum a shot to relax him and very gently put the tubing up inside Nahum's nostril and worked it back down toward his stomach. Slowly Brian forced water up the tube, hoping to dislodge the blockage. Even with the tranquilizer it was hard to hold Nahum. He reared back. Brian tried again. Nahum reared up and almost fell sideways. After five abortive attempts, Brian was worried. "I'm not sure how much this little old guy's heart can take." He suggested that we let Nahum rest for a few hours and see if the water had in fact worked. He told me to call him in a couple of hours and let him know what was happening.

I led Nahum to a large clean stall across the barn and went back to get Solomon. He was lying down and did not want to get up. "Poor little guy," said Brian, "his arthritis is really bothering him." He showed me how by using the base of Solomon's tail as a handle he could lift him to a standing position. "Even a large cow or heavy horse can not resist that pressure and will stand up," he told me.

"Brian," I said, "if Nahum dies, Solomon must go too. They can not be separated now."

"Yes, they are old buddies," he agreed. "They will go together, I promise."

Solomon followed Nahum to the stall. Each step of the way was painful. I stayed with them for a while hoping to see some improvement as I stroked them and rubbed the base of their ears, their favorite caress. The two little old fellows just looked old and forlorn.

In an hour they seemed to be resting more comfortably. Nahum's nostrils were clear, and he breathed quietly. When I went out an hour later, Nahum was dead lying on his side. His heart must have just stopped. He had not been gone long. His soft ears and face were warm. Still on my knees I hugged Solomon's neck, burying my face in his fur. "I'm sorry, I'm sorry." I could not tell anything from Solomon. He just stood there, his lifelong friend at his feet. I looked across the barn to where the other ten donkeys were standing side by side with their heads over the partition watching. They knew.

Thinking it might help to keep Solomon warm through the cold lonely night, I gave him a generous portion of grain. I knew he would be joining Nahum long before it could do him any harm. He ate it deliberately as if in a trance. I gave him a little more and he ate that. I went into the house and called Brian.

Yesterday morning after surgery, Brian's assistant Steve came. He knew all the donkeys well.

"I'll hold Solomon for you," I said.

"Will you be okay?" he asked.

"Yup" I answered, but tears came anyway when Solomon dropped to the floor under my hands. The two little donkeys lay peacefully together.

In the late afternoon I waited in the barn for Mark Thompson to come and bury them. While I waited I carried bales of hay and buckets of water, preparing the main stall so the donkeys could come in and not witness the burial. My hands and feet were numb with cold. As I moved around the barn, I thought I heard startling sounds coming from the stall where Nahum and Solomon lay. At first I could not believe my ears. It took me just a minute, and then I understood. As Solomon's body contracted in the fierce cold, the warm gasses from all the grain in his stomach were being forced through his intestines and out. It was an eerie sound, and I thought to myself the Song of Solomon continues but in a different key.

That was yesterday. It is cold again today. The donkeys are on the south side of the barn sheltered from the wind accepting gratefully whatever warmth they get from the pale winter sun. As I sit here in my study and look across the frozen pond and up the ice and snow-covered field beyond, I know how lonely winter can be. But if I shut my eyes, I can change it all to early summer. The soft grass ripples in the wind and wild iris punctuate the marshy places by the pond. I can hear the sound of frogs and bird songs, and up on the hill beyond the donkeys are grazing contentedly. If I call them, "hey fellows," they will lift their heads and there will be a chorus of braying answering me. If I call again, they will turn and come trotting, cantering down the hill to the barn eager to know what the next adventure will be.

But today, the cold is cruel and the wind blows.

EPILOGUE

When it came time to leave Highland Farm, it was not hard to find good homes for the donkeys. Molly and Madeline went to a family in Massachusetts. Hanna and Jenny went to one in Vermont and Nicholas Nye to a family in southern New Hampshire. The rest, Susie, Shaggs, Jessica, and Emma all went to a large breeding farm for thoroughbred horses. Those excitable animals often find reassurance in the company of donkeys. It is not unusual to see a docile donkey traveling with an excitable horse or waiting with one before it competes. Old Annie, Nahum, Solomon, and Mupo are all buried and rest in peace at Highland Farm.

Following Herb's death, Mozart and I moved to Jackson, Mississippi, where Harriet and her husband lived. Mozart sat on my lap all the way as Harriet and I drove south, and he was unfazed by the motel in Troutville, Virginia, where we spent the night. Mozart's final years were in Jackson where he was happy, first in the company of a marvelous tricolor female, Hibou (who really did look like an owl). When sadly she died, he put up with two black kittens, Hither and Yon. Mozart died in his fourteenth year. His ashes are in the peaceful small graveyard near Highland Farm where Herb's are.

Many years have passed since we all left Highland Farm. The people who live there obviously love it. It is a farm in name only now. The fences are all gone, and what were the pastures are now neatly mown lawns stretching up through the orchard to the woods beyond. Along the edge of the road are handsome new stonewalls, four stones wide. How those early settlers would have coveted such barriers for their cattle! The noble barn is empty of animals and so is the large field behind it.

Living now in the South, I still look for donkeys. They make me smile. On Route 49 near Collins, south of Jackson, there used to be a big field with about twenty donkeys of different colors. They looked like a herd roaming the southwest. Once I stopped at the house, and the man told me he rented his field to the person who owned the donkeys. I asked if we could go out and see them. He agreed and together we went through the gate. "Watch where you walk," he said. "Sometimes there's rattlers here." The donkeys looked up as we approached, curious but not yet ready to be friendly. They were a herd, and people at best were an intrusion. They moved off down the field. But it was nice to be in their midst for a moment. The following year the donkeys were gone, and crops grew in their place.

I am amazed at how many donkeys I do see as I drive from my home, now in Memphis, to Kentucky or Boston or out to Wyoming, and I wonder why other people have them. Are they guards against coyotes? Are they companions for children or horses? Do they come in the house when the grownups are gone? Do they make people smile?

A photo of Jenny sits on my desk, but it is the donkeys at Highland Farm that I dream about, and I wake up disoriented, still feeling their fur on my hands.

978-0-595-38855-4
0-595-38855-8

CPSIA information can be obtained at www.ICGtesting.com
Printed in the USA
LVOW06s2214050114

368207LV00001B/181/A